And When You Pray...

Prayer Journal

By: Dioveris Lopez

For more information, please write to:
Dioveris Lopez
Email: dioverisartistry@gmail.com

Dedication

This book is dedicated to Jesus Christ, my daughter, mother, spiritual mother, Next Dimension and the Body of Christ.

Lord Jesus, you're the reason I'm alive. You're the reason I can truly live now. Your Spirit is the reason I keep going when I can't in my own strength. Your hand Lord, was on my life from before I was in my mother's womb and you have unveiled my eyes to the truth. I am free so that others may be set free. I pray, Lord, that this is just the beginning of the liberty you've meant for us to live in. You get all the Glory, Honor and Praise. I love you.

Elise, this is for you, too! My goal in life is that you and those after you would never have to endure what I had to, what grandma had to, and those before her. I pray that you know the Lord. I pray that He's the center of your life and through and in Him you live. You are precious, special and are meant to be here. You will have a voice in this world because the Lord meant for it to be so. He said the fruit of my womb is blessed- that's you. I love you.

Mom, thank you. Thank you for who you are. You taught me to be transparent, vulnerable and to not be afraid to be myself. You've taught me how to handle persecution, shame and guilt. You taught me how to love unconditionally. You taught me how to go to the Lord. You never forced Him on me and pointed me to Him in a peculiar way, I thank you. I thank God for your resilience, faith and perseverance. I hope you are proud. I love you.

Bonita, you listened to the Father, picked me up from a low place and doctored me up. You saw in me what I didn't see myself. When I thought I was dying, you knew I was truly about to live. You've always pointed me to the Lord and that taught me a valuable lesson. You guide me in my faith, in prayer, self-care, love, integrity, and so much more. Legacy-you are truly living in it and the fruit of your labor is manifesting. I love you.

Next Dimension, yawwwwl, God knew what He was doing when He put us together. I'm so happy and blessed to have a community of powerful godly women like yourselves. May this be a ripple effect in our circle! You've seen me at my lowest, my weakest and my strongest. This is for you too. I love you.

Lastly, the Body of Christ. We suffer with Christ that He may get the glory. Thank you for laying your life down and being an example of what love looks like. I encourage you to keep dying to live- that's a true leader. To every person who saw me, believed in me, trusted me, listened to me, edified me and prayed for me. This is for you too. I love you.

Contents

Intro

You know, it's been a struggle to start and finish this. Every time I walk into a new season and assignment, what I thought I had down-packed shows to not be so. When God takes you from Glory to Glory, the faith and belief that worked in the past season is desolate in the new one. At least that's how my journey has been thus far. I get so desperate for God and I fight to not give up.

My name is Dioveris Lopez. Right now, I'm a twenty-eight year old Prophetess. I have been given the gift to be bold as a lion but I'm as soft and fragile as a lamb. I've been given the gift of being a mother. I've been given the gift to love and be passionate. I've been given the gift to speak with conviction and I've been given the gift to be vulnerable and transparent. I love to evangelize, teach, counsel and hold others accountable.

I wondered how in the world this prayer journal was going to be any different than anyone else's. Then I was told, "Only you can deliver the way you do to the fish God has assigned to your life. A million prayer books can be written and these people will not be able to receive the message until they get it delivered the way you deliver it." So here it is. I am nothing without Jesus. I am not doing this in my own power but by His grace and Spirit. I give Jesus all the glory and I pray you are able to hear Him, see Him, experience Him and love Him more through these prayers.

Just know that you don't have to hide from God. I know, it's hard. It's hard when you have lived your life hiding but the truth is, our heavenly Father wants us to come to Him like He intended for us in the Garden of Eden. Because of Jesus, we have that freedom again. When you read these prayers, read them out loud. We live by faith and not by sight. Faith comes from hearing and hearing by the word of God. So allow yourself to hear truth. Drown out the lies you've been feeding yourself thus far. When you're done praying, read the referenced bible verses and then just sit in our Father's presence as He speaks back to you; and be patient. Write down your thoughts, use the blank spaces to draw or doodle.

Allow yourself to build this relationship with the Father who yearns for this moment with you. Commit yourself to Him. You must hunger and thirst for His righteousness; I promise your life will never be the same.

God bless you and please, receive.

"But when ye pray, use not vain repetitions, as the heathen do: for they think that they shall be heard for their much speaking. Be not ye therefore like unto them: for your Father knoweth what things ye have need of, before ye ask him."
Matthew 6:7-8

What is prayer?

Dictionary.com states that Prayer is a solemn request for help or expression of thanks addressed to God or an object of worship. Let's keep it simple: Prayer is a conversation with God, your heavenly Father. You should be praying to God the Father, He wants a relationship with you. If you're not, we'll talk about that at the end of this introduction.

Prayer can be hard. Especially when you don't know what to pray, or how to pray, or when to pray. We overthink everything in our human nature. The truth is, in our own nature we cannot do it. We'll give up "because the carnal mind is enmity against God: for it is not subject to the law of God, neither indeed can be." Romans 8:7. We must rely on the Spirit of God to help us. He knows our needs and promises to supply them all according to His riches and glory by Christ Jesus. Philippians 4:19.

I started seeking a deeper relationship with God in September of 2018. Prior to September of 2018, I would maybe pray for 5 minutes a day- either before bed or when I woke up. I realized recently, after being more intentional, that I always spoke to the Lord but it was only when I needed something. To be honest, I always needed something. Now, I have learned to give Him my attention, listen for His voice and surrender to Him fully. My prayer time doesn't look the same all of the time. Sometimes, I sit with my legs crossed and speak to God. Other times, I get on my knees with my face to the ground and cry out. I sit with intentional quietness or write my prayers out in a letter to the Father. There's no religiosity to it. I just surrender to the Lord, come to Him in truth, desperation and love. Sometimes my time with the Father lasts an hour and sometimes my time with Him is 10 minutes of surrender.

The purpose of this book, is to usher you into prayer. My hope is that you are led to a more vulnerable place with God because the truth is, Jesus died for the sins of man. The sin and the shame that Adam and Eve opened the door and chose to walk in was defeated at the cross. No need to feel scared, ashamed, or guilty about anything. God loves us so much that He came up with a new plan (gave His only begotten Son) that we may live and experience a true and everlasting relationship with Him. So, if you believe it, then receive it.

If you've never surrendered your heart and/or your life to the Lord Jesus Christ and you feel a conviction within, you know, like He's calling you? Repeat the following prayer out loud and step into the next dimension of your life.

Salvation Prayer

Father,

I've tried it all. I've done everything under the sun in this world seeking satisfaction that I have yet to find. I'm heavy. I'm tired. I feel scared sometimes. Sometimes I feel insecure. I'm lost a lot of the times but your Word says that Jesus died on the cross so that I don't have to carry these things anymore. In 1 Peter 2:24, you said that He himself bore our sins" in his body on the cross, so that we might die to sins and live for righteousness, that "by his wounds" we "have been healed." Lord, I'm ready to die to sin. I'm ready to die to myself and live in Christ Jesus. I believe Christ died on the Cross. I believe He rose on the third day. I believe that He is seated at your right hand and I declare Jesus Christ to be Lord over my life.

Lord, I repent of my sins; known and unknown and I receive your Holy Spirit now to do a greater work in me and through me. Father, please, do it for your glory. I will follow you (again), Jesus. I pray this in Jesus' mighty name. Amen.

Fear

Father,

Here I am. I'm not sure where or how to start but I'm here. I'm not afraid to enter into the throne of grace because I need you. I am nothing without you.

Father, In Jesus name, though I am not afraid to enter into your presence, I am full of fear. The fear that reverences you and the fear to live. Scared because what if this is my last day? I know, it sounds crazy and your word says you haven't given me a spirit of fear but of power and of love and a sound mind. In the world, I would be diagnosed. I would be judged but ultimately you are the judge. As much as I am strong in myself, I am weak. Thank you that when I am weak is when I am really strong because of YOU, Jesus. Thank you that your grace is sufficient for me. God, I thank you for your word that is true. Your word says no weapon formed against me shall prosper. It says that the weapons of our warfare are not carnal but are mighty through pulling down strongholds. It also, that the battle isn't mine, that it's yours and. I choose to be in your presence right now, Father, believing and receiving that you will take it from here. I trust that you will turn it all around for my good and for your glory. You've done it before Lord, so, would you please do it again? Lord, you are a wonderful God, a beautiful God, and a mighty and strong tower. You are the solid rock upon which I stand. You and no one else but you gives me life. Jesus, you are so graceful and loving. You're patient and kind. You are love. You give me what I don't deserve and what I can't work for. Thank you for being who you are. You show me you love me, over and over again. You love me even when I can't love myself and try to hide. You won't leave me. You won't forsake me.

Your love is unconditional and for that I'm thankful and I am expectant. Thank you for your Spirit that is alive in me now. I pray this all in the name of my mighty King and Savior, Jesus Christ. Amen.

For God has not given us a spirit of fear, but of power and of love and of a sound mind.

2 Timothy 1:7

Count to 3 as you take a deep breath in and let it out slowly as you count to 7. Sit quietly. Do you see or hear anything? Write your thoughts on the following pages.

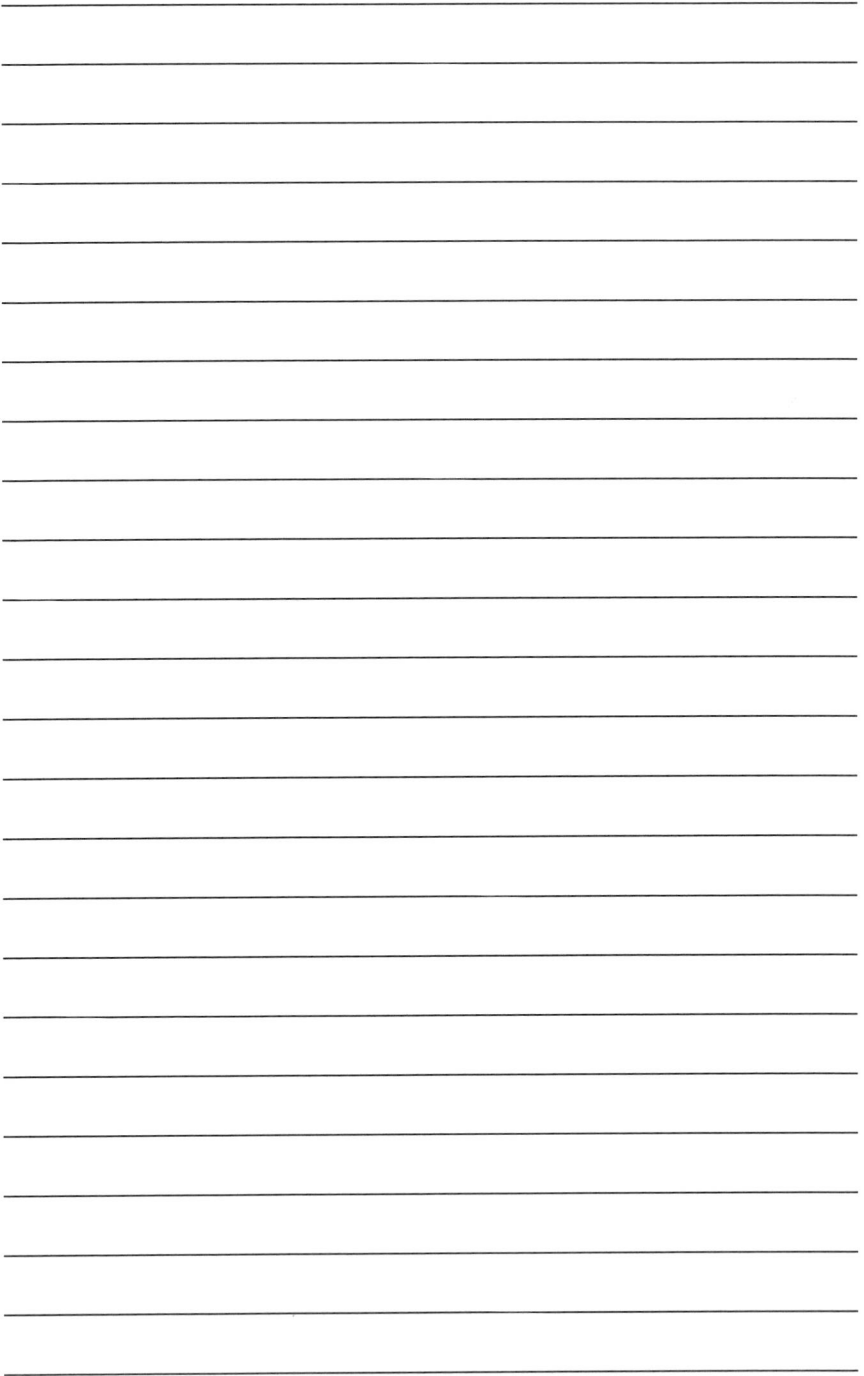

And He said to me, "My grace is sufficient for you, for my strength is made perfect in weakness." Therefore most gladly I will rather boast in my infirmities, that the power of Christ may rest upon me. Therefore I take pleasure in infirmities, in reproaches, in needs, in persecutions, in distresses, for Christ's sake. For when I am weak, then I am strong. I have become a fool [a]in boasting; you have compelled me. For I ought to have been commended by you; for in nothing was I behind the most eminent apostles, though I am nothing.
2 Corinthians 12:9-11

Count to 3 as you take a deep breath in and let it out slowly as you count to 7. Sit quietly. Do you see or hear anything? Write your thoughts on the following pages.

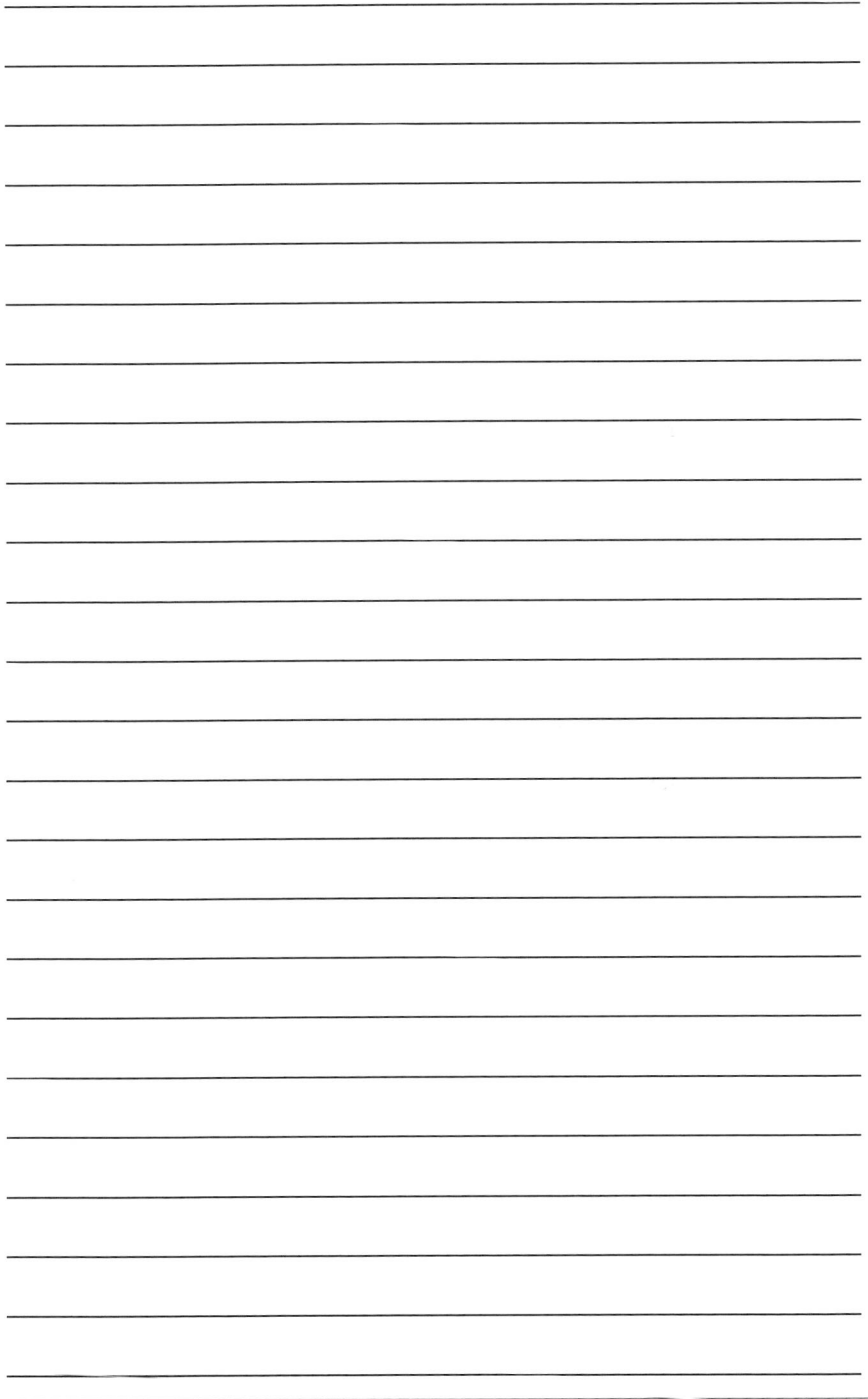

And he said, "Listen, all you of Judah and you inhabitants of Jerusalem, and you, King Jehoshaphat! Thus says the LORD to you: 'Do not be afraid nor dismayed because of this great multitude, for the battle is not yours, but God's. 2 Chronicles 20:15

Count to 3 as you take a deep breath in and let it out slowly as you count to 7. Sit quietly. Do you see or hear anything? Write your thoughts on the following pages.

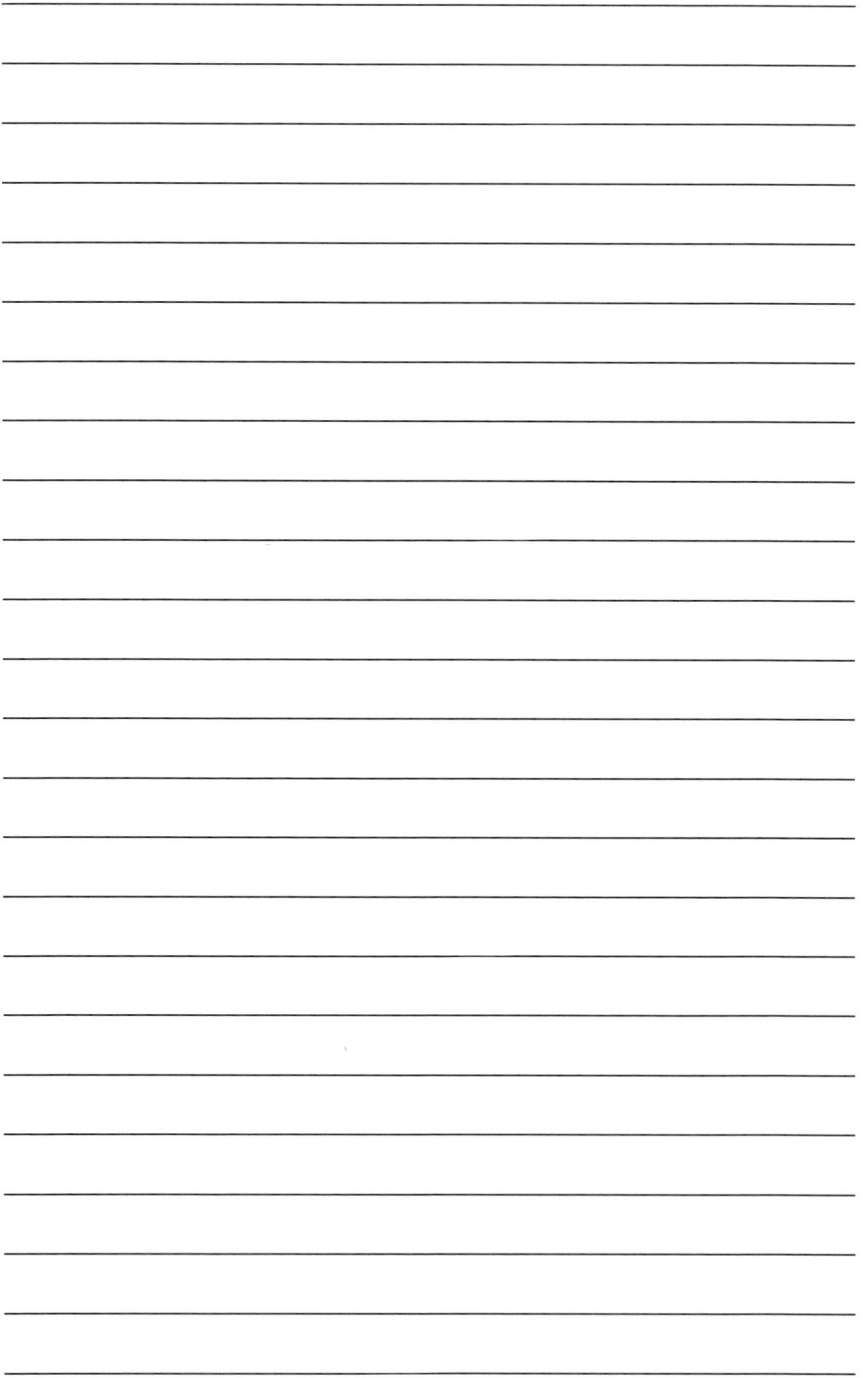

For the weapons of our warfare are not [a]carnal but mighty in God for pulling down strongholds.
2 Corinthians 10:4

Count to 3 as you take a deep breath in and let it out slowly as you count to 7. Sit quietly. Do you see or hear anything? Write your thoughts on the following pages.

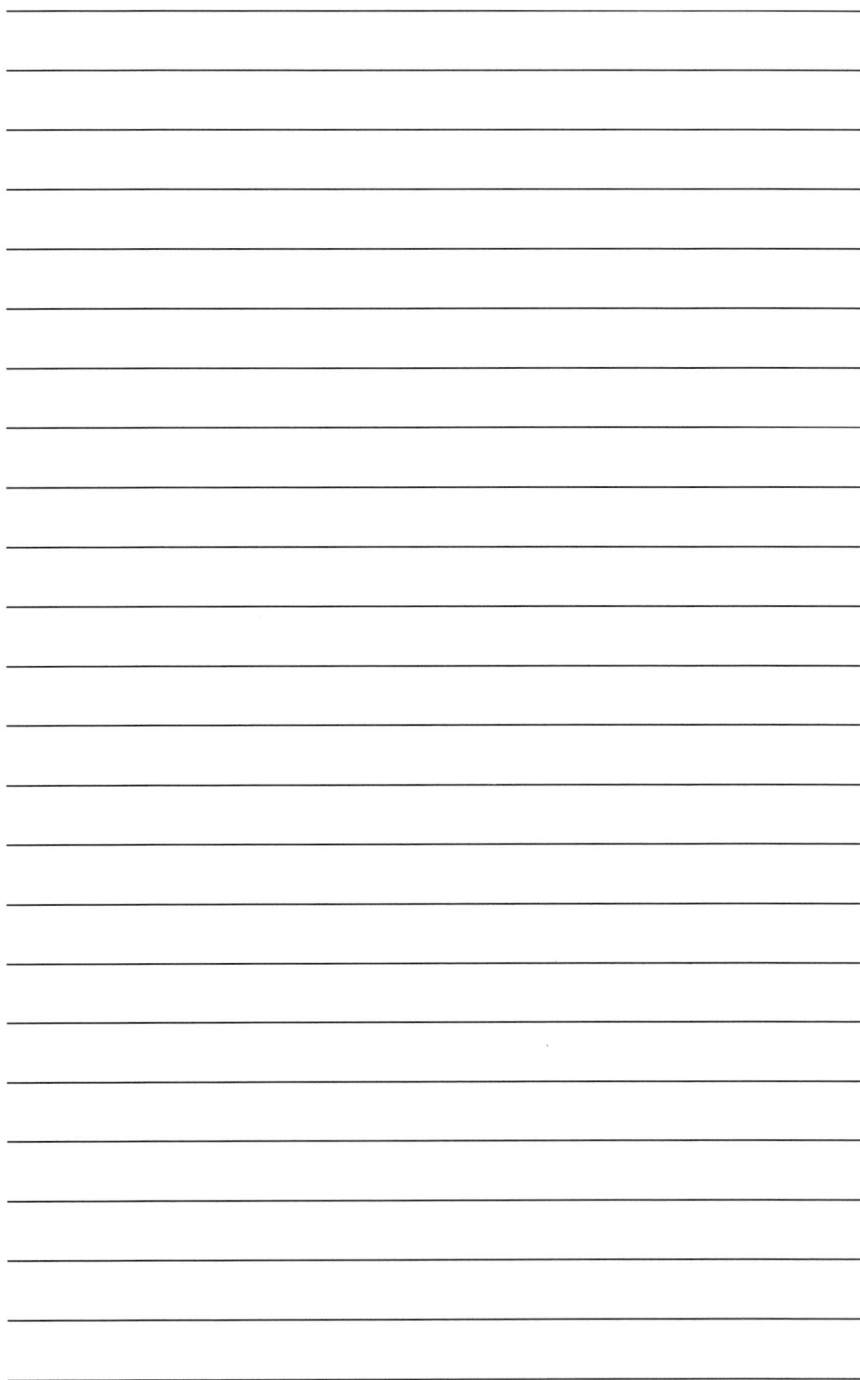

Prophetic Prayer:
Times, Seasons and Process

Father, I thank you! I thank you for the tiny testimonies. Help me be aware of your Holy Spirit who surrounds me. He is omnipresent and omnipotent. Father, help me see you in what seems like the smallest things. Help me see you when the birds are chirping joyfully and help me see You in how they fly and are always together. Thank you for those who support me and always stay by my side. The birds worry not about what they will eat. They trust you. They know you will provide. Thank you for the signs, Father. The trees, flowers and grass, they trust you. They grow according to the season. Lord, in the winter, the trees are bare but they stand strong. They weather the storms, God. In the fall, the trees don't hold on to the leaves that should fall off. God, they let go, trusting in the new season to come. Father, in the spring, the trees flourish. They are bright, colorful and fruitful. They understand the times and seasons more than I do! Thank you Father for how you show me life, in life. The things in this world that you gave me dominion over, trust you more than I do. Oh, how I want to be more obedient, more trusting. Holy Spirit, would you help me? God, you show me through butterflies, that the process is so important. A butterfly cannot be born before it's time and season. Caterpillars even understand the times and seasons. They obey when the season has come for them to just eat. Help me understand the seasons- when it's time for me to just be in your presence or to be still and be fed by your word. Help me understand when it's time to rest and trust you like a caterpillar in its third stage. In the third stage, the outside of the cocoon looks like nothing is changing but the work is being done on the inside. Help me understand when it's a time of resting and trusting you. Help me to wait and be in tune with you. I want to be able to recognize when it's time for me to fly. And when it's time to fly, help me accept that there's a process in learning how to fly. Father, I want to be so intentional in life. I want to do your will and nothing else. Help me, as I pick up my cross daily, to live for you. Let the whole world know how great you are through me. Use me for your glory, Father.

You're so gracious. So loving and kind. So thoughtful and careful in how you even created life. Who would be so kind to give the answers? If we stop, be still and look around us, we will see that you have given us all the signs and answers we need; in the seasons, in the life of insects, in landscape; in the life of Jesus; the model and example of who we are to be. Thank you for giving your life for us dear Lord. You love me so much, that you died and endured all I would have had to, so that I may live for eternity. I press on towards the mark, Jesus. Let your Kingdom come in my heart and give me the eyes to see as you do, Lord. Give me the ears to hear as you do and give me a deeper revelation of your word, your plan and a deeper revelation of who I am in you, Jesus. It's all in your perfect timing. And it's all for your Glory. Let all men know I've been walking with you. Let them all see. Let no man deny you are the Lord of lords and King of kings.

In Jesus', sweet and precious name I pray,
Amen.

To everything there is a season, A time for every purpose under heaven: A time to be born, And a time to die; A time to plant, And a time to luck what is planted; A time to kill, And a time to heal; A time to break down, And a time to build up; A time to weep, And a time to laugh; A time to mourn, And a time to dance; A time to cast away stones, And a time to gather stones; A time to embrace, And a time to refrain from embracing; A time to gain, And a time to lose; A time to keep, And a time to throw away; A time to tear, And a time to sew; A time to keep silence, And a time to speak; A time to love, And a time to hate; A time of war, And a time of peace.
Ecclesiastes 3:1-8

Count to 3 as you take a deep breath in and let it out slowly as you count to 7. Sit quietly. Do you see or hear anything? Write your thoughts on the following pages.

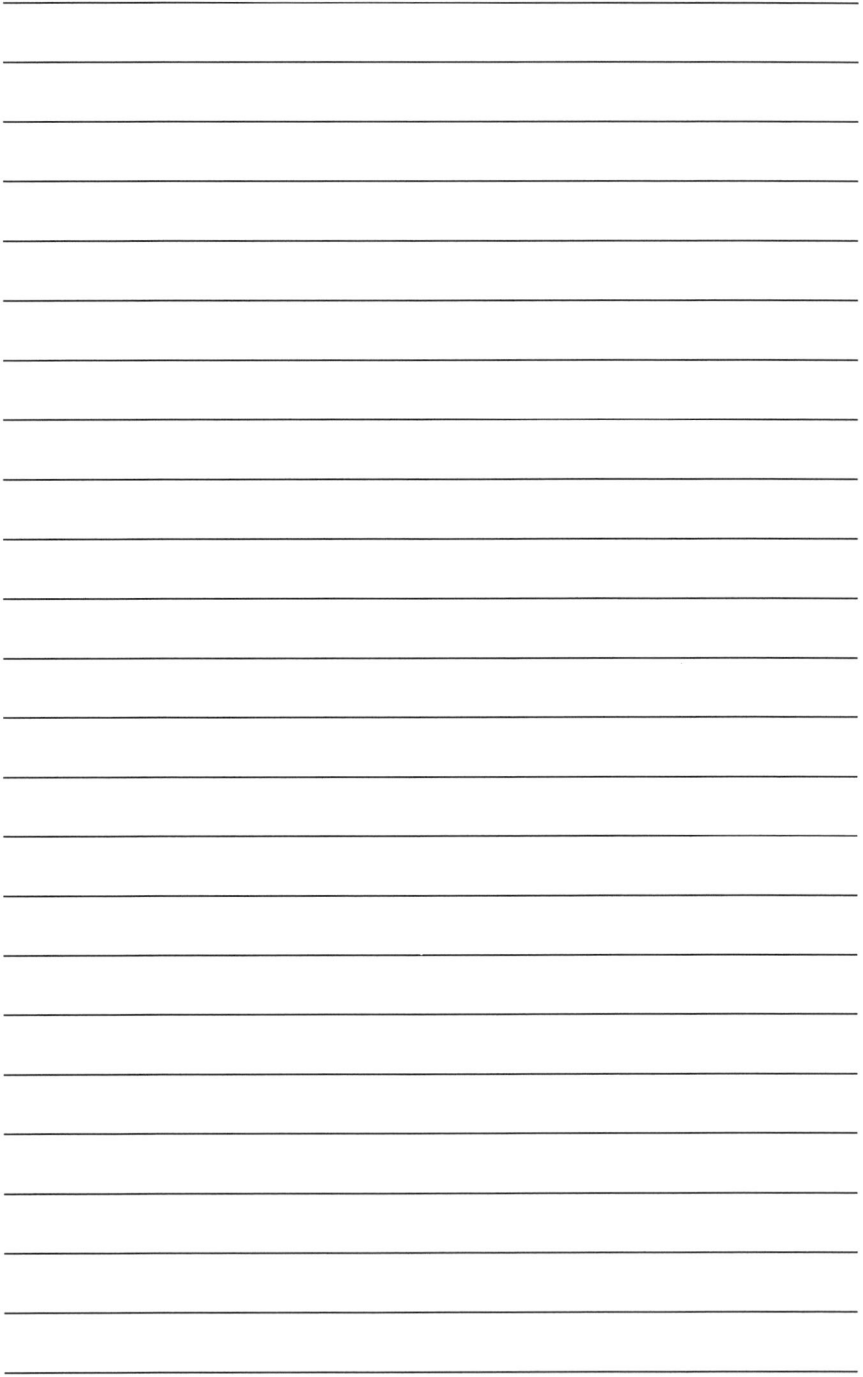

Look at the birds of the air, for they neither sow nor reap nor gather into barns; yet your heavenly Father feeds them. Are you not of more value than they?
Matthew 6:26

Count to 3 as you take a deep breath in and let it out slowly as you count to 7. Sit quietly. Do you see or hear anything? Write your thoughts on the following pages.

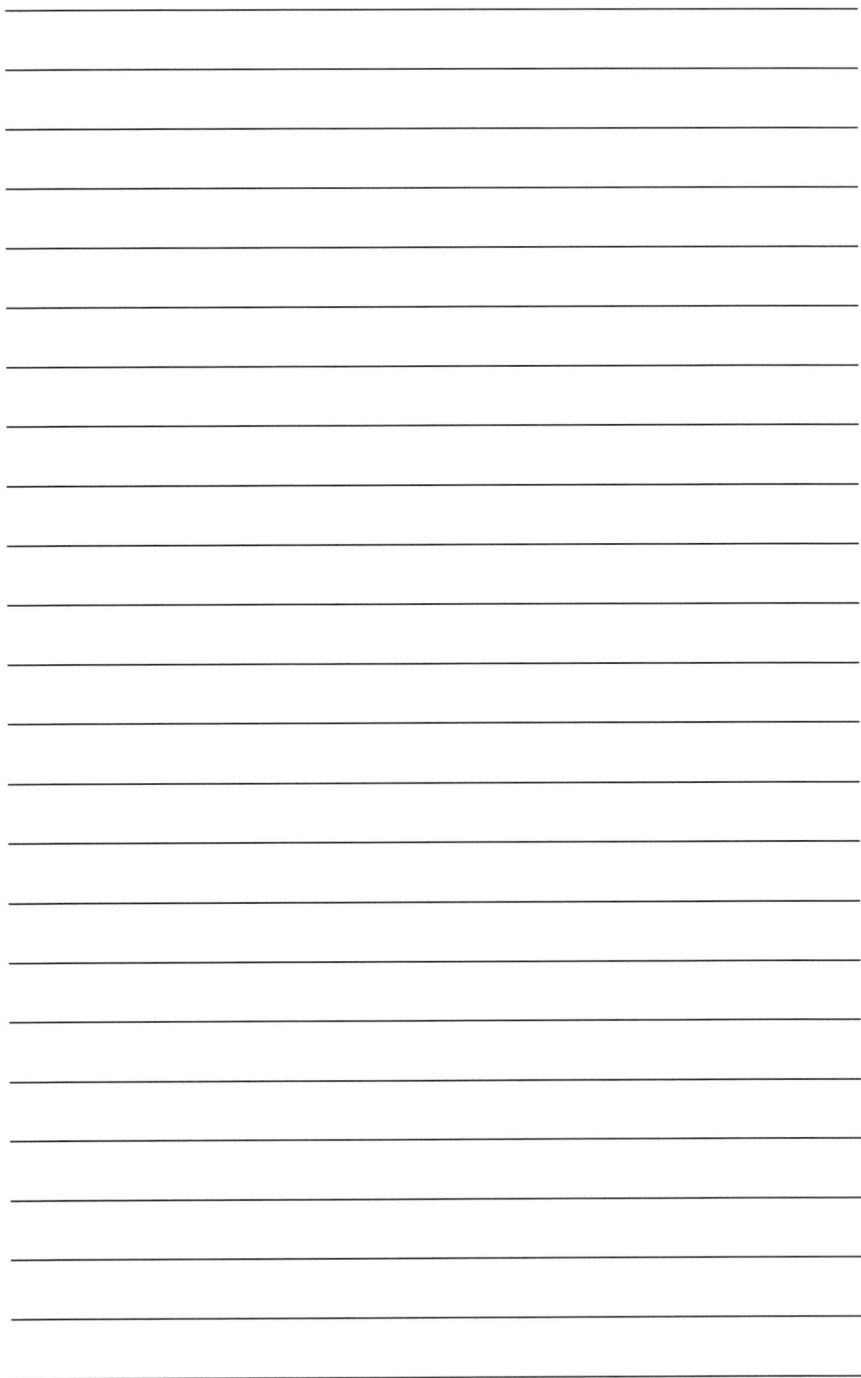

Then He said to them all, "If anyone desires to come after Me, let him deny himself, and take up his cross [a]daily, and follow Me.
Luke 9:23

Count to 3 as you take a deep breath in and let it out slowly as you count to 7. Sit quietly. Do you see or hear anything? Write your thoughts on the following pages.

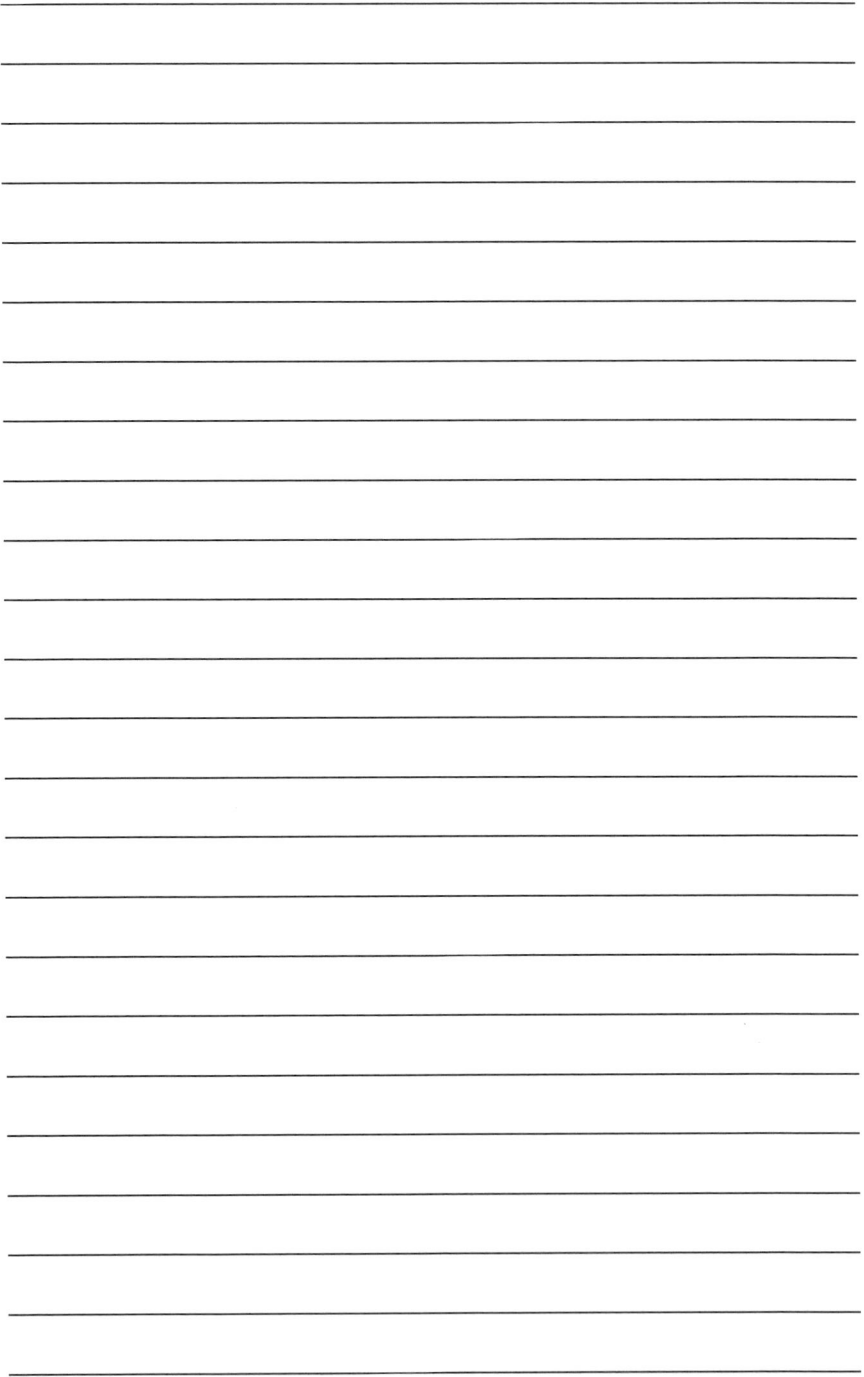

For God so loved the world that He gave His only begotten Son, that whoever believes in Him should not perish but have everlasting life.
John 3:16

Count to 3 as you take a deep breath in and let it out slowly as you count to 7. Sit quietly. Do you see or hear anything? Write your thoughts on the following pages.

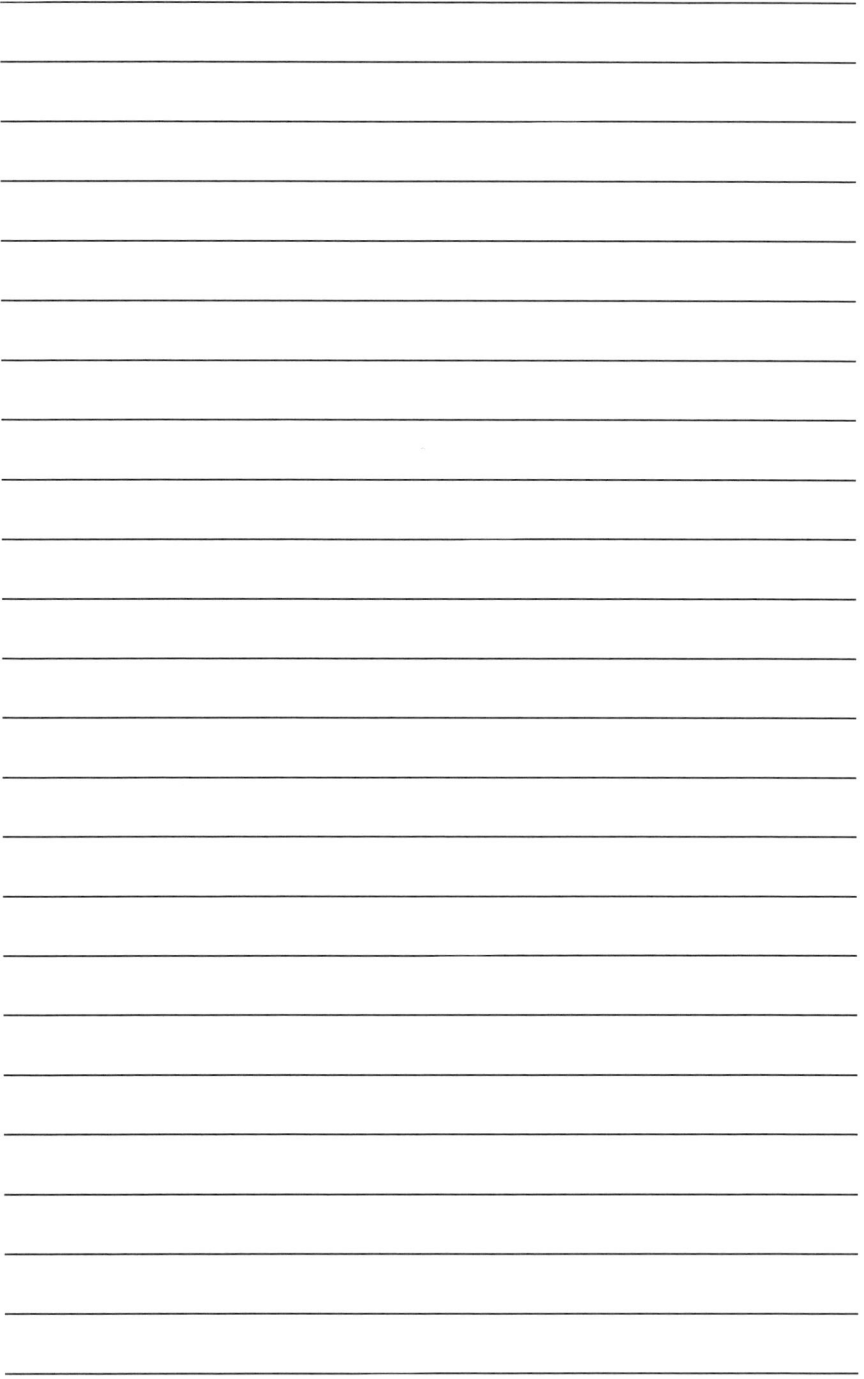

Your kingdom come. Your will be done on earth as it is in heaven.
Matthew 6:10

Count to 3 as you take a deep breath in and let it out slowly as you count to 7. Sit quietly. Do you see or hear anything? Write your thoughts on the following pages.

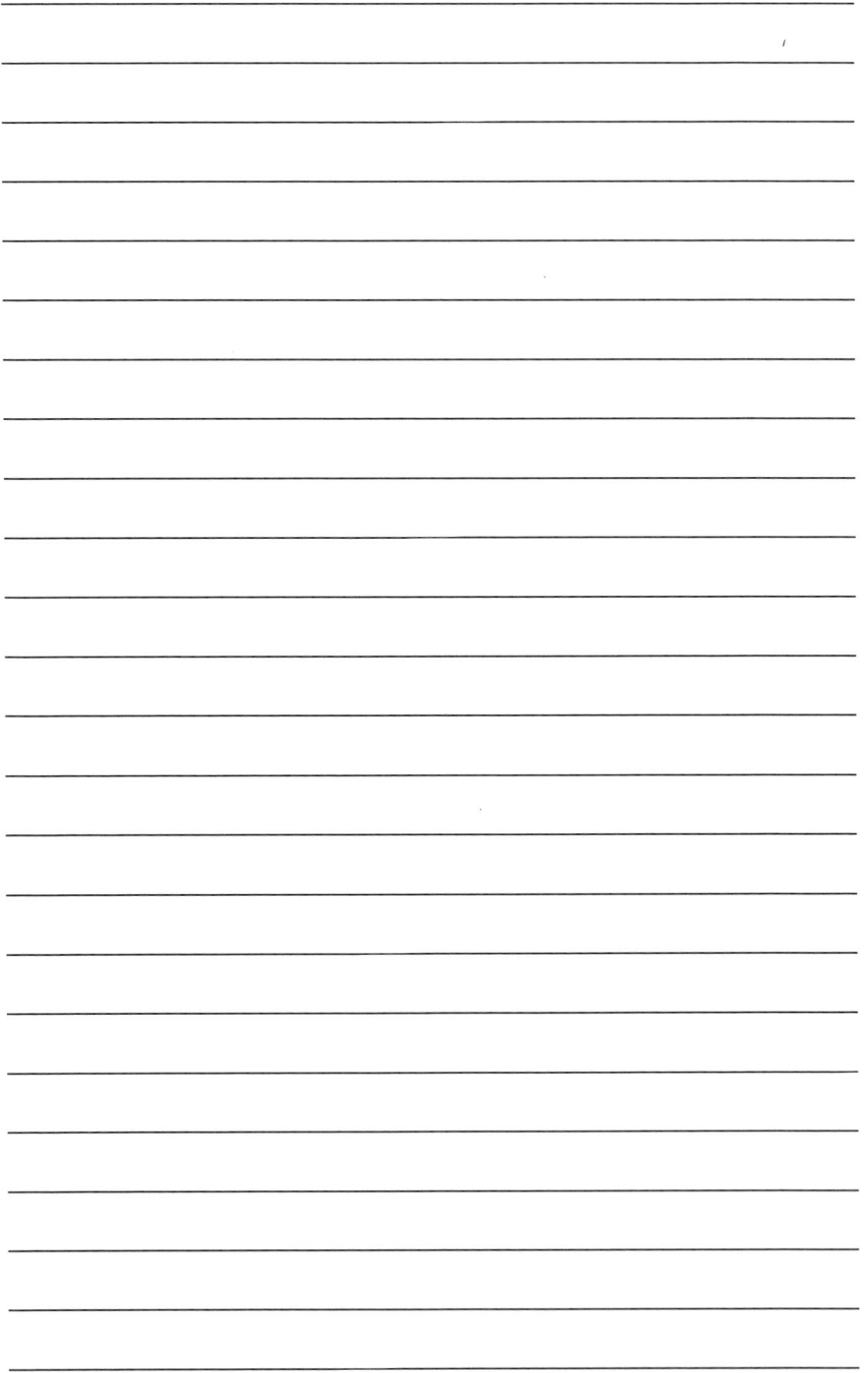

I press toward the goal for the prize of the upward call of God in Christ Jesus. Therefore let us, as many as are mature, have this mind; and if in anything you think otherwise, God will reveal even this to you.
Philippians 3:14-15

Count to 3 as you take a deep breath in and let it out slowly as you count to 7. Sit quietly. Do you see or hear anything? Write your thoughts on the following pages.

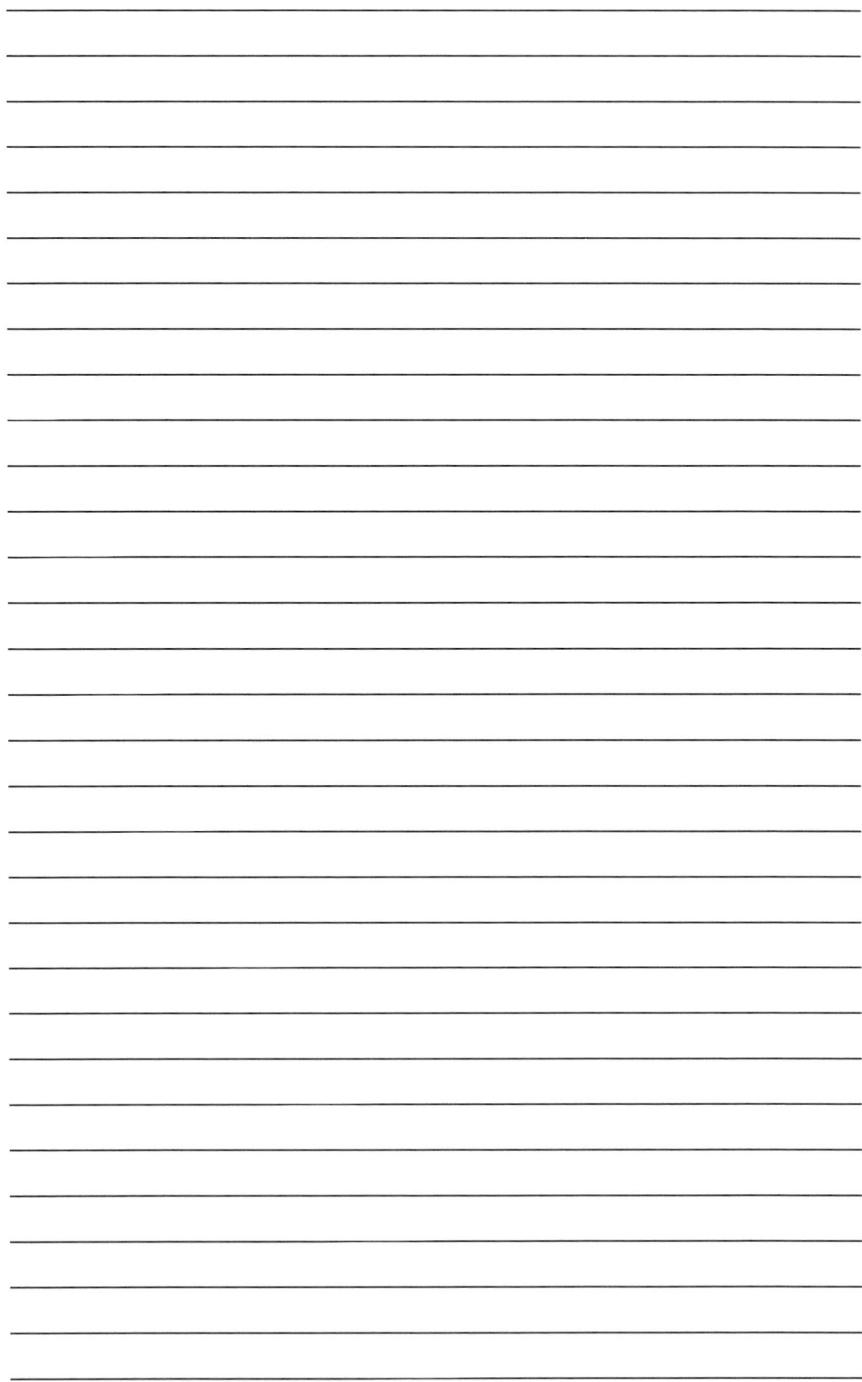

Surrender, Repentance and Deliverance

Abba, Father.

Thank you for being my lover and my friend.
Thank you for coming to earth in human form so that you would know what it's like to live a life like mine. Lord, You, who knew no sin, became sin. You're a God who understands my pain, my temptations to give up and my temptations to give in. You're a God who has seen what I see but whose ways are not like mine; whose thoughts are not like mine. You're a God who gives what we ask for if we believe.

Lord, I have tried it all. Sex, money and drugs. I have tried to fit in to a world that I am not of. I have been hurt, disappointed, deceived and used over and over again. I have allowed the sun to go down on my anger. I have swam in the pool of self-pity. All that you have told me not to do, I have done. That was before I knew that it would do me no good.

I have tried it all in myself. God, nothing compares to living for you. Though it is painful, it is rewarding. Father, as you know, I still am tempted to hold grudges, to be entitled, to be prideful- and sometimes I open the door to these things before I even recognize it.

Lord, all I know is to confess my sins to you. I don't know how to fix it all and I know I cannot. Only you can fix it, by your Holy Spirit, who I love and recognize as a manifestation of you.

I want to be in relationship with that part of you even more.

I want to be friends with you, Holy Spirit. I want to be comforted by you and acknowledge you for it. I want to hear your whisper when you speak what the Father speaks. I want to share my day with you and partner with you as I seek God and worship sweet Jesus.

I cannot do it alone and I recognize that. I know I try it often without even realizing it.

I know that you are with me and you have worked through me and in me before. But I don't want to be in and out of this thing with you. I want to live in the Spirit. I want to walk, talk, and display Jesus by your power.

Hear my heart, God. Cleanse my heart, Oh God. Would you please give me a fresh infilling of your powerful Spirit? I cry out to you now. Give me more and deeper utterance. Let the evidence show. Let me body spark from head to toe with evidence of your power in me. Father let demons scatter as I go where you send me because of your Holy Spirit in me. Let me preach and teach your word with boldness. Give me the gift of prophecy. Help me see, hear, smell, touch, speak, perceive. Father, I desire the gifts of the Spirit and I desire the fruit of the Spirit. I desire to serve you every second of the day. I desire to please you. Would you grant it to me? I believe you can. I believe it is your will. I receive the anointing. I give you glory. I welcome your glory. I await your voice even now.

I worship you mighty God.
I glorify you.
I shout Hallelujah and I give you my all.
I surrender to you.
Have it all.
Have my emptiness and fill me up.
Have my sorrow and give me Joy.

Have my anxieties and cares because you care for me.
I give you my shame and guilt in exchange for your peace
I repent for holding on to this longer than I had to.
I repent for idolizing sin, knowingly and unknowingly.
I want to be free and I renounce all things unlike you.
I renounce sexual immorality, lust, and control.
I renounce fear, guilt and shame.
I renounce unforgiveness and grudges.
I renounce all soul ties and come out of agreement with the devil who I resist NOW in the name of Jesus.
I repent Lord.
I renounce rebellion, which is as sinful as witchcraft therefore I renounce witchcraft as well.
I release myself from these things with the power and authority you've given me. In Jesus Name.

Lord, may your Holy Spirit fill me up. Arise in me. Fill all voids, Lord, and areas in me which have been emptied. May fire rise from the depth of my soul for you-from you. May everything unlike you burn now, in the name of Jesus. Renew my mind, Holy Spirit. I receive my freedom now. In Jesus name. Your word says you gave me the authority to trample upon serpents and scorpions and I used the authority you've given me now. The enemy is under me feet because I am seated in Heavenly places with You, Oh Lord. Send your angels, Father, to fight for me, to heal me, to minister to me. Open up my spiritual eyes that may I see what you've done and are doing.

I have said it and it is so. In Jesus name.

"For my thoughts are not your thoughts, neither are your ways my ways," *declares the LORD.* *Isaiah 55:8*

Count to 3 as you take a deep breath in and let it out slowly as you count to 7. Sit quietly. Do you see or hear anything? Write your thoughts on the following pages.

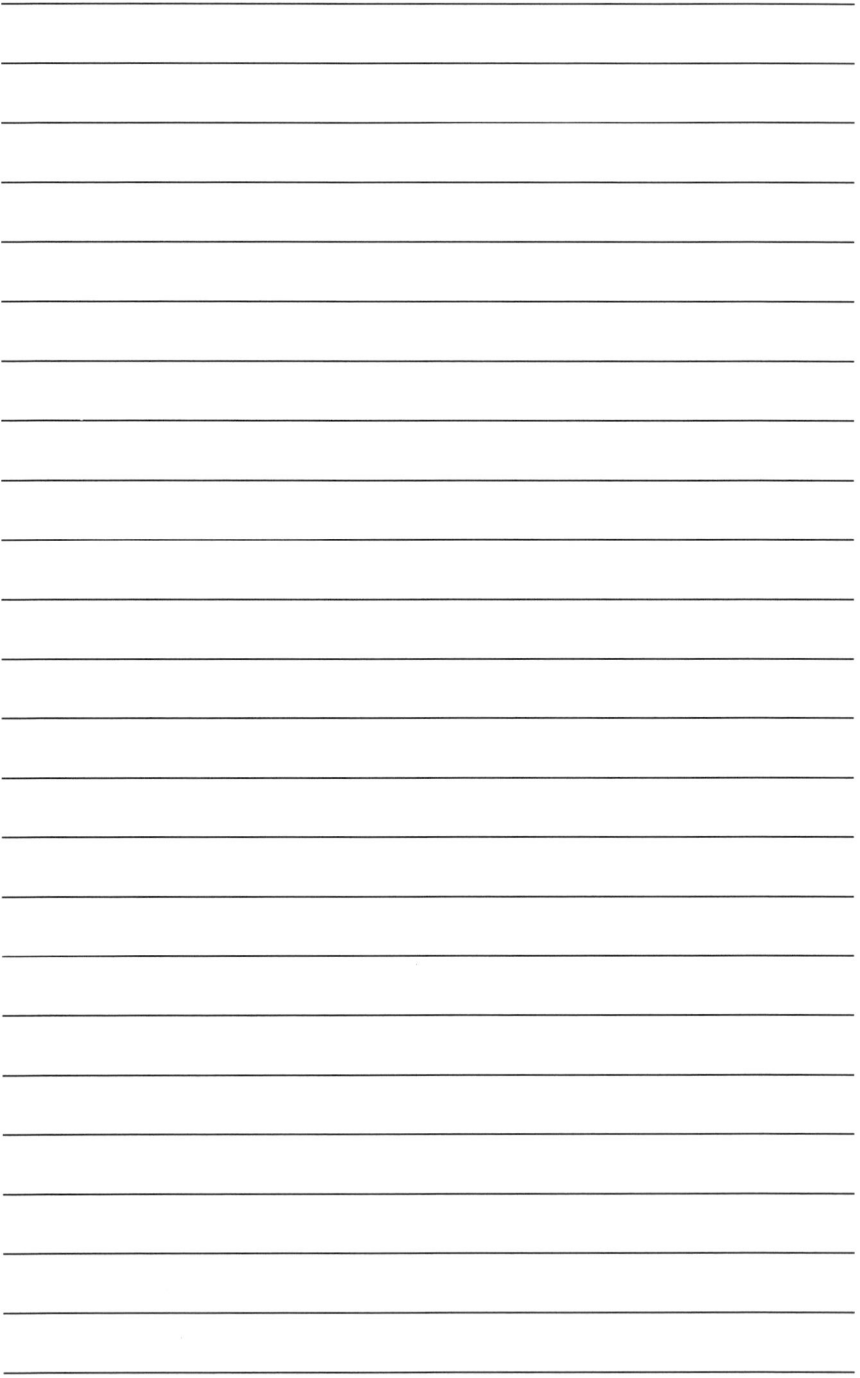

God made him who had no sin to be sin for us, so that in him we might become the righteousness of God.
2 Corinthians 5:21

Count to 3 as you take a deep breath in and let it out slowly as you count to 7. Sit quietly. Do you see or hear anything? Write your thoughts on the following pages.

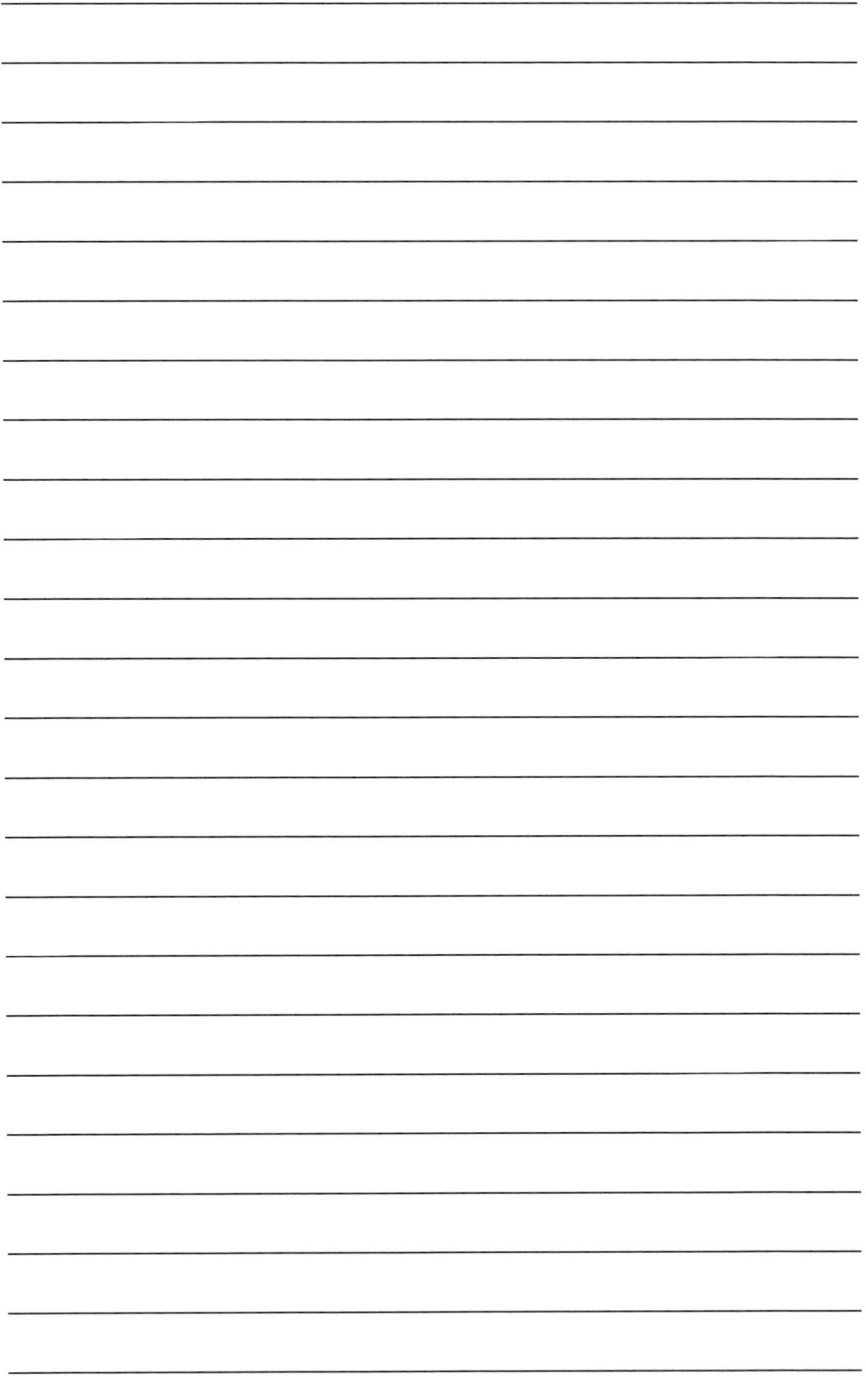

Therefore I tell you, whatever you ask for in prayer, believe that you have received it, and it will be yours.
Mark 11:24

Count to 3 as you take a deep breath in and let it out slowly as you count to 7. Sit quietly. Do you see or hear anything? Write your thoughts on the following pages.

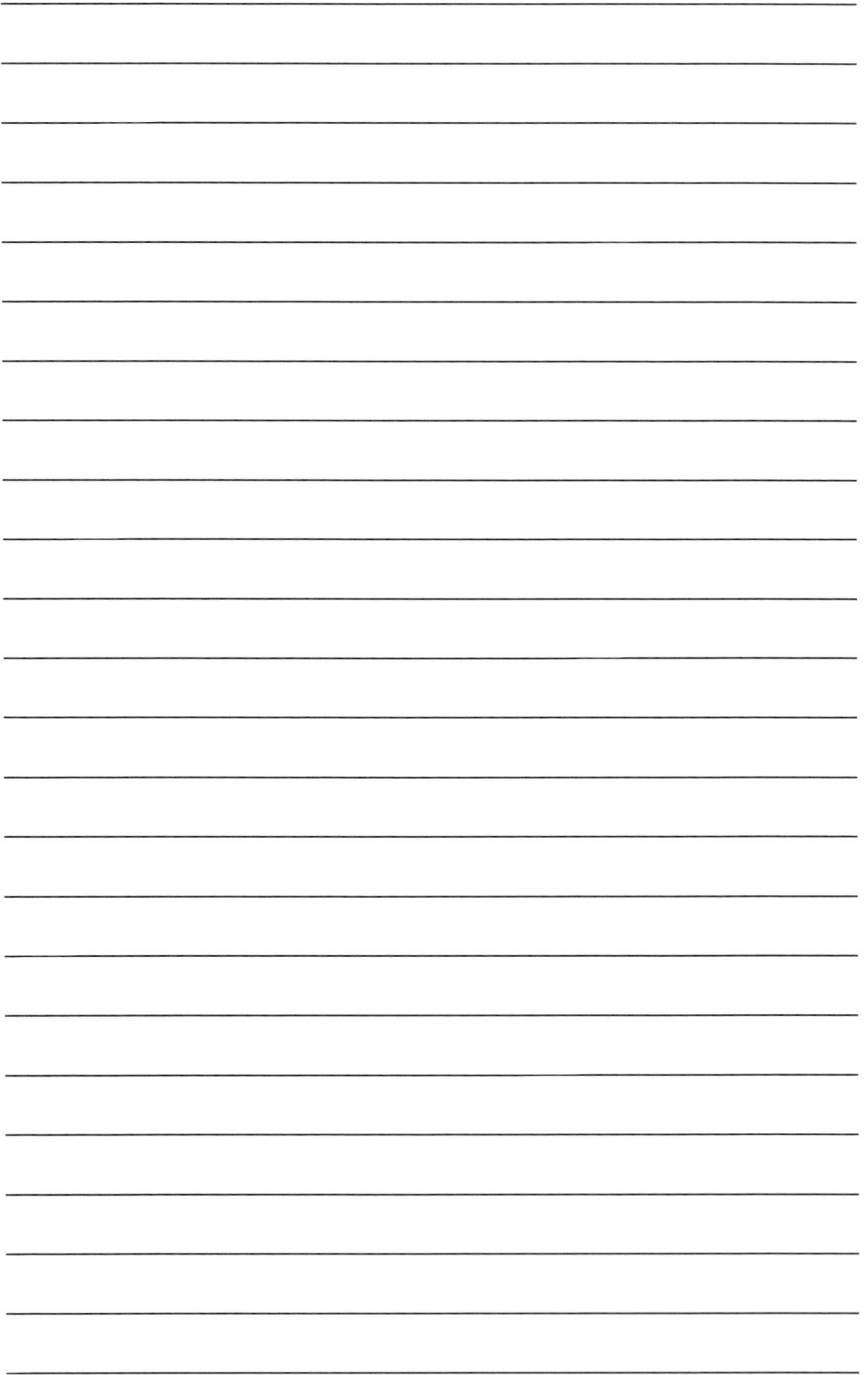

"In your anger do not sin": Do not let the sun go down while you are still angry.
Ephesians 4:26

Count to 3 as you take a deep breath in and let it out slowly as you count to 7. Sit quietly. Do you see or hear anything? Write your thoughts on the following pages.

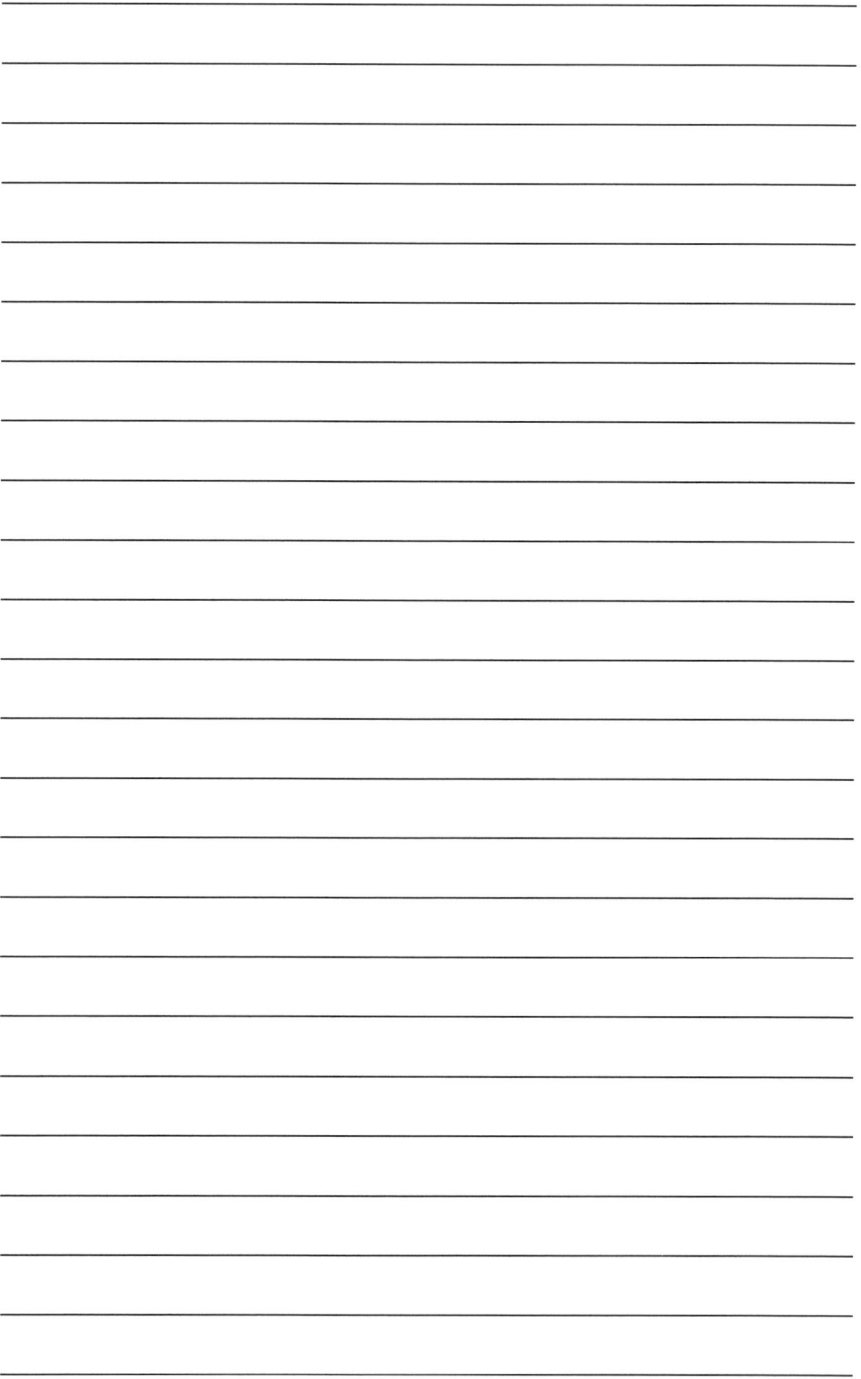

For we live by faith, not by sight.
2 Corinthians 5:7

Count to 3 as you take a deep breath in and let it out slowly as you count to 7. Sit quietly. Do you see or hear anything? Write your thoughts on the following pages.

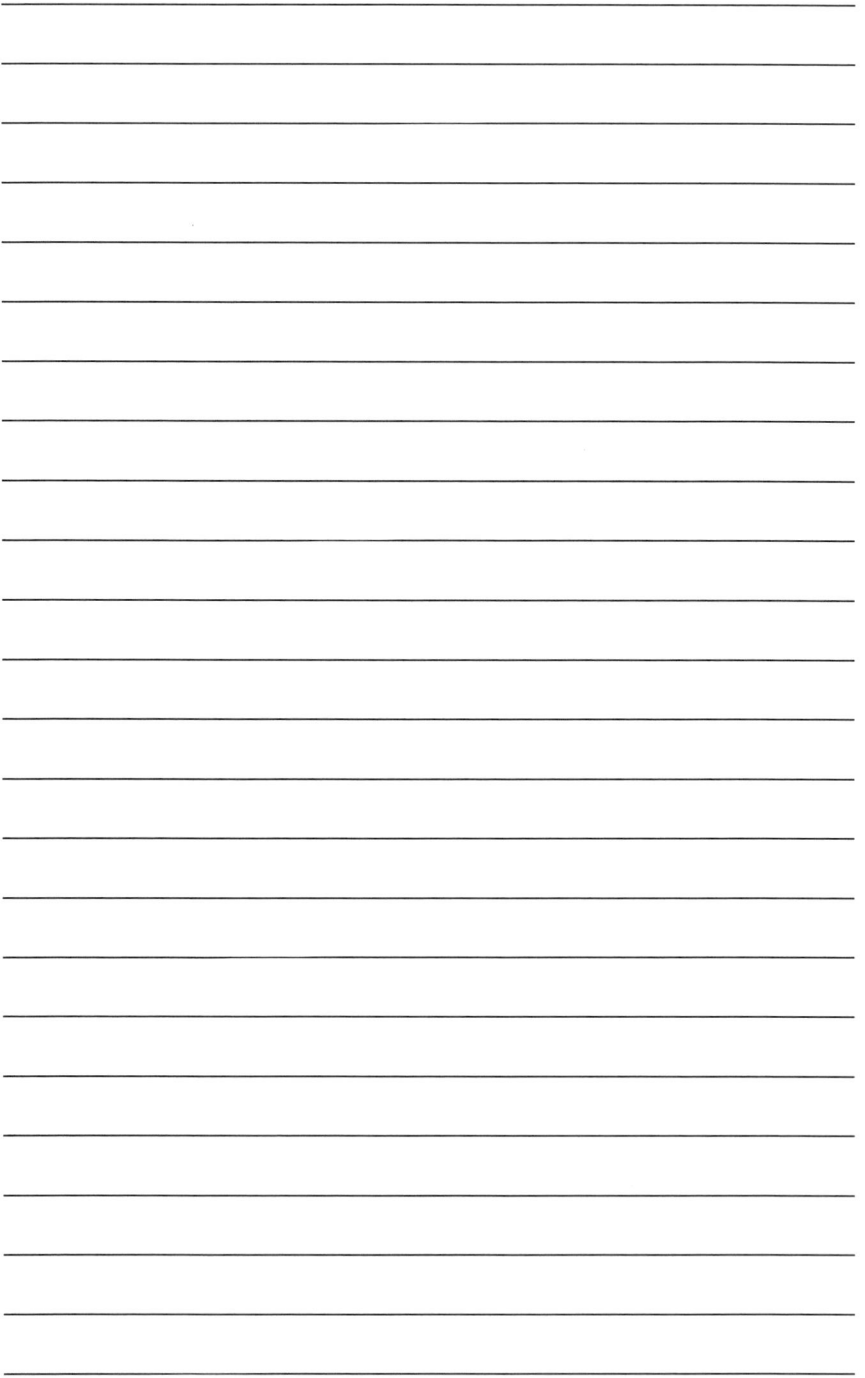

The Word became flesh and made his dwelling among us. We have seen his glory, the glory of the one and only Son, who came from the Father, full of grace and truth.
John 1:14

Count to 3 as you take a deep breath in and let it out slowly as you count to 7. Sit quietly. Do you see or hear anything? Write your thoughts on the following pages.

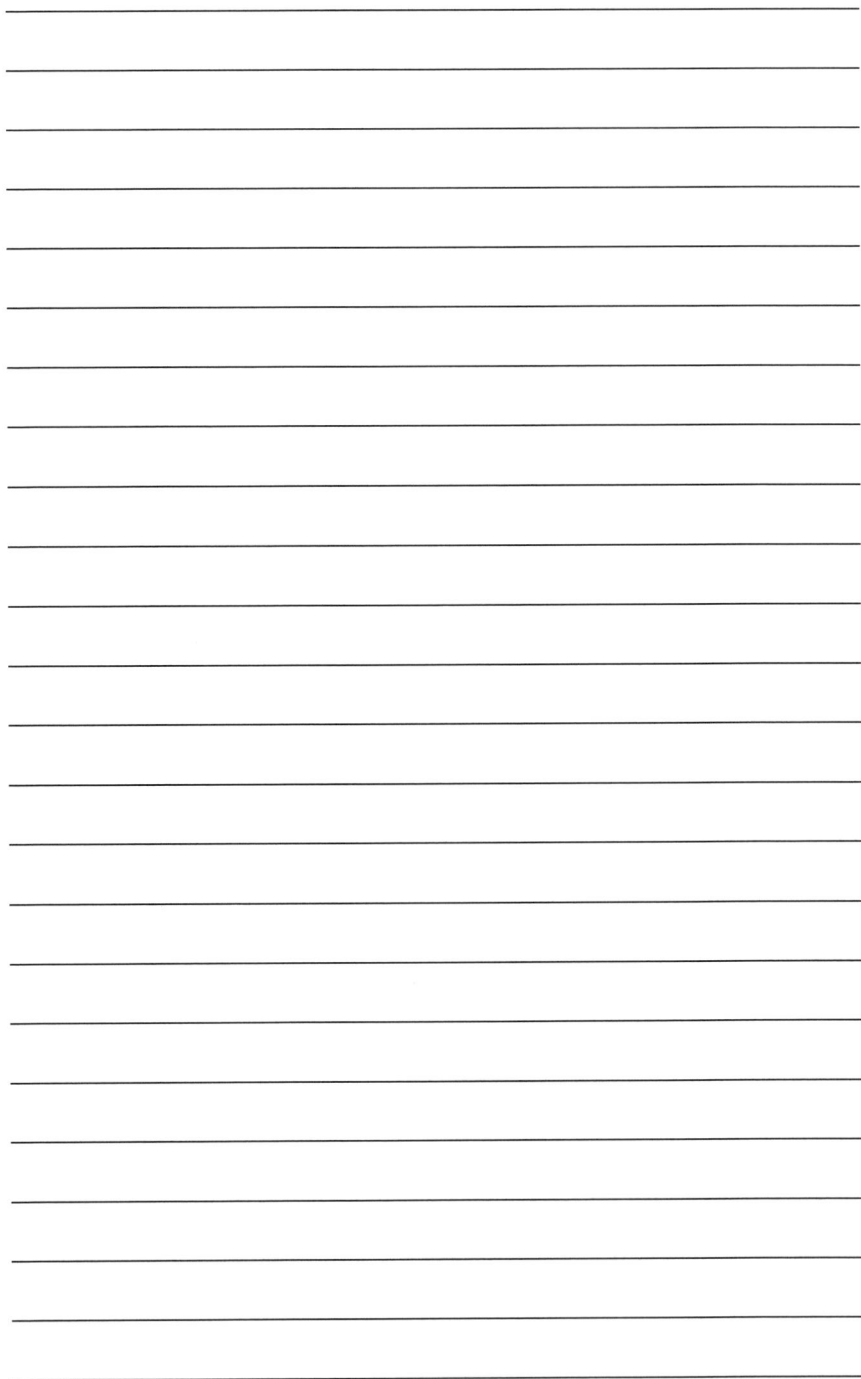

For we do not have a high priest who is unable to empathize with our weaknesses, but we have one who has been tempted in every way, just as we are--yet he did not sin.
Hebrews 4:15

Count to 3 as you take a deep breath in and let it out slowly as you count to 7. Sit quietly. Do you see or hear anything? Write your thoughts on the following pages.

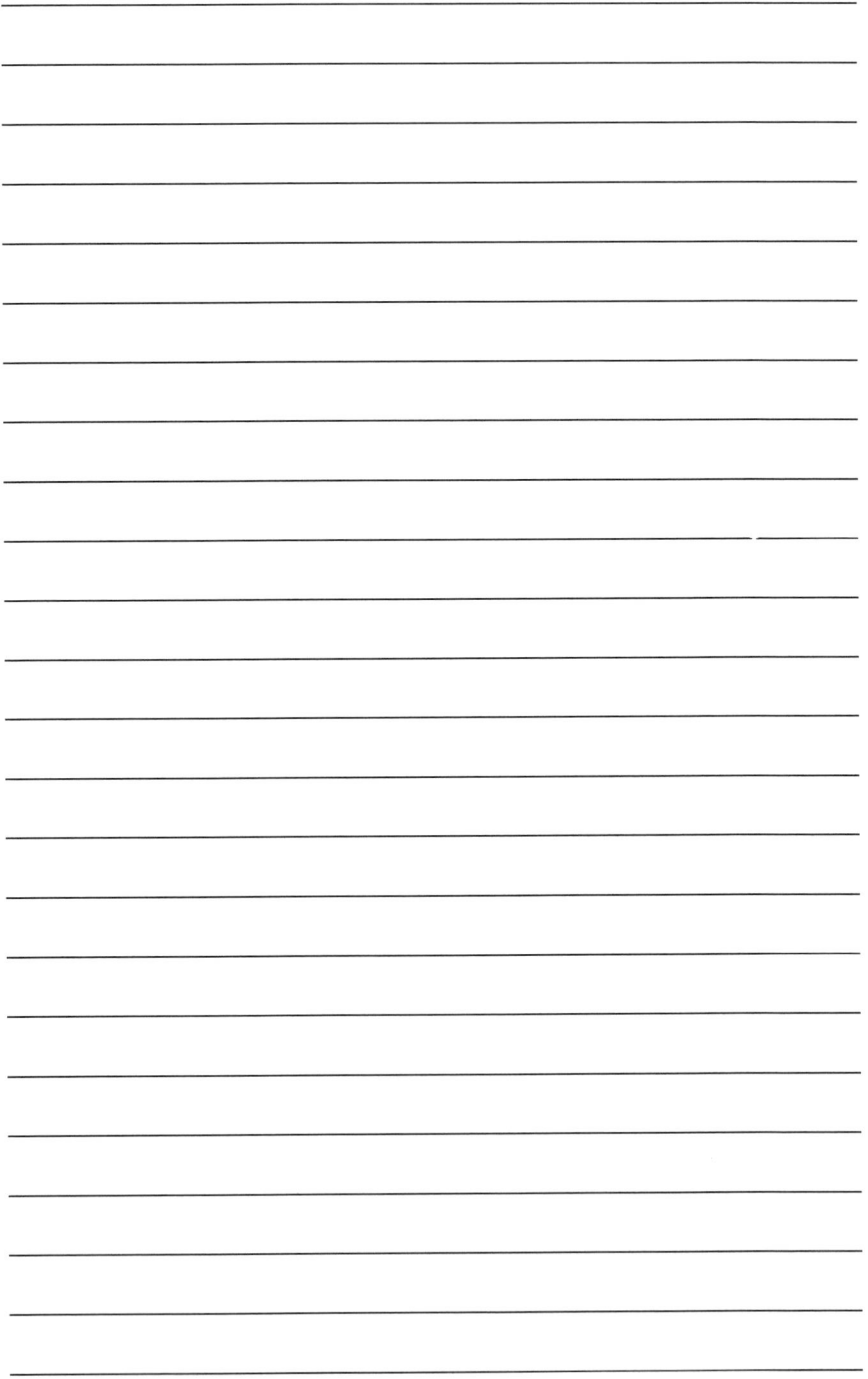

Yet if you devote your heart to him and stretch out your hands to him.
Job 11:13-15

Count to 3 as you take a deep breath in and let it out slowly as you count to 7. Sit quietly. Do you see or hear anything? Write your thoughts on the following pages.

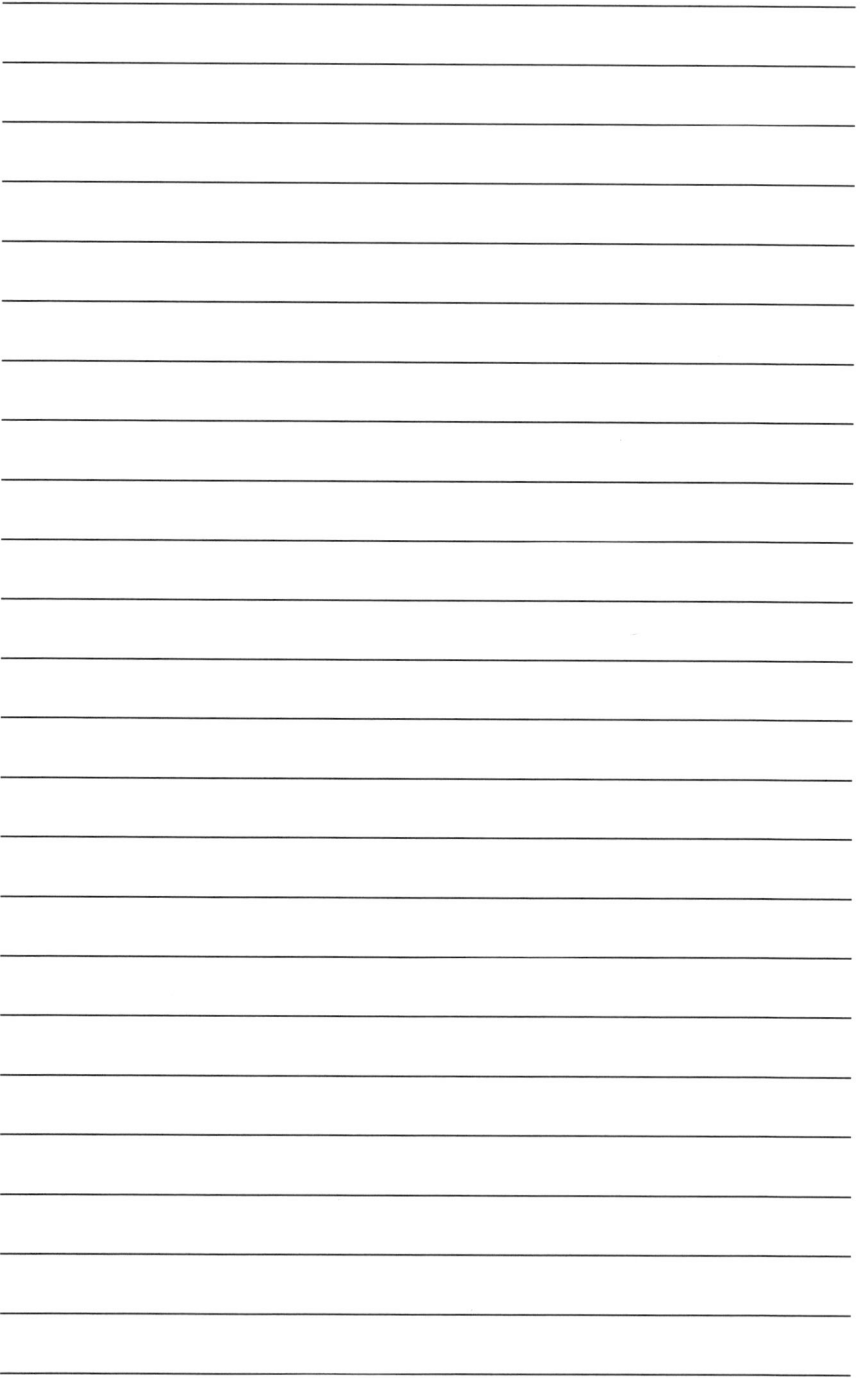

But the fruit of the Spirit is love, joy, peace, forbearance, kindness, goodness, faithfulness, gentleness and self-control.
Galatians 5:22-23

Count to 3 as you take a deep breath in and let it out slowly as you count to 7. Sit quietly. Do you see or hear anything? Write your thoughts on the following pages.

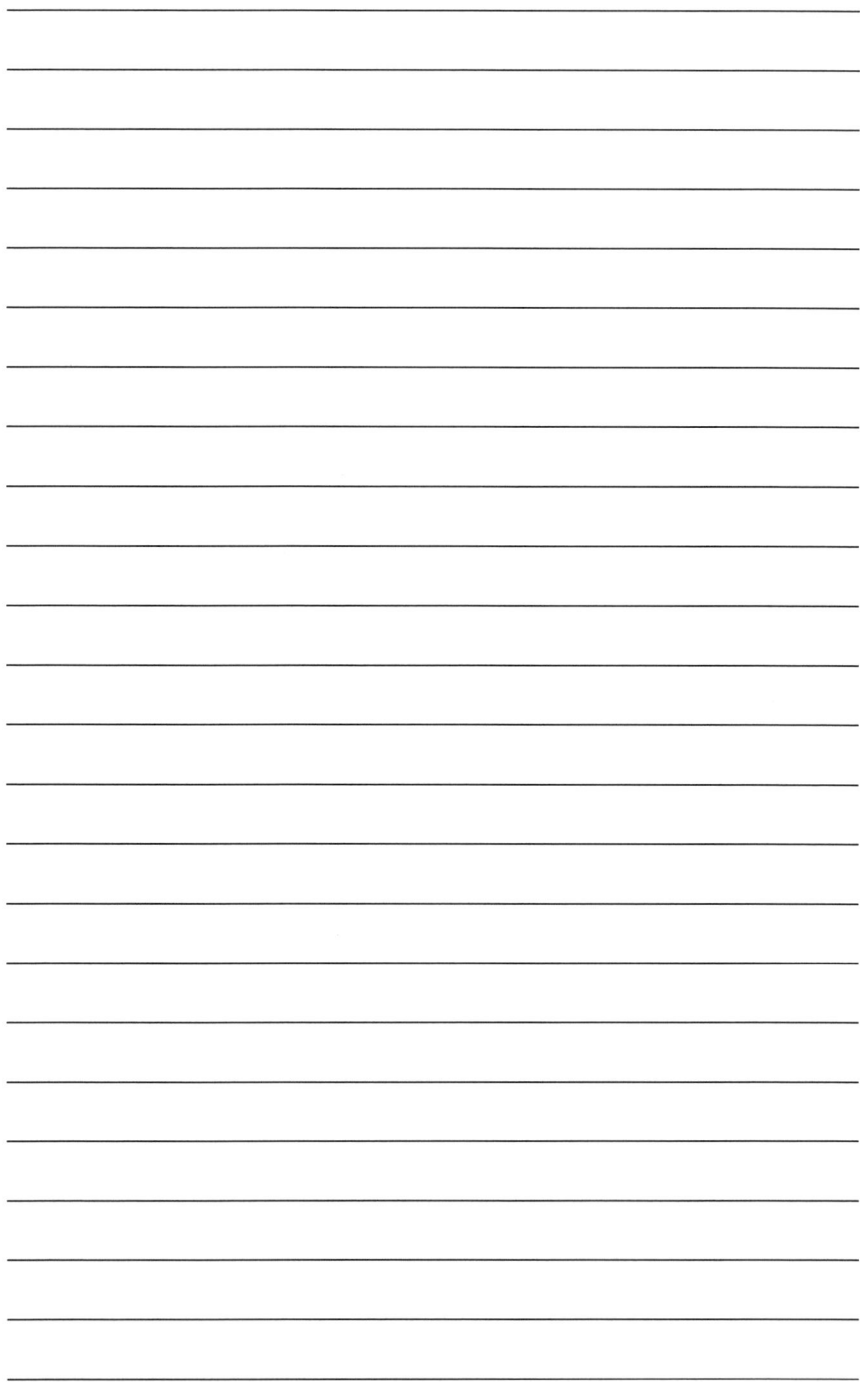

All of them were filled with the Holy Spirit and began to speak in other tongues as the Spirit enabled them.
Acts 2:4

Count to 3 as you take a deep breath in and let it out slowly as you count to 7. Sit quietly. Do you see or hear anything? Write your thoughts on the following pages.

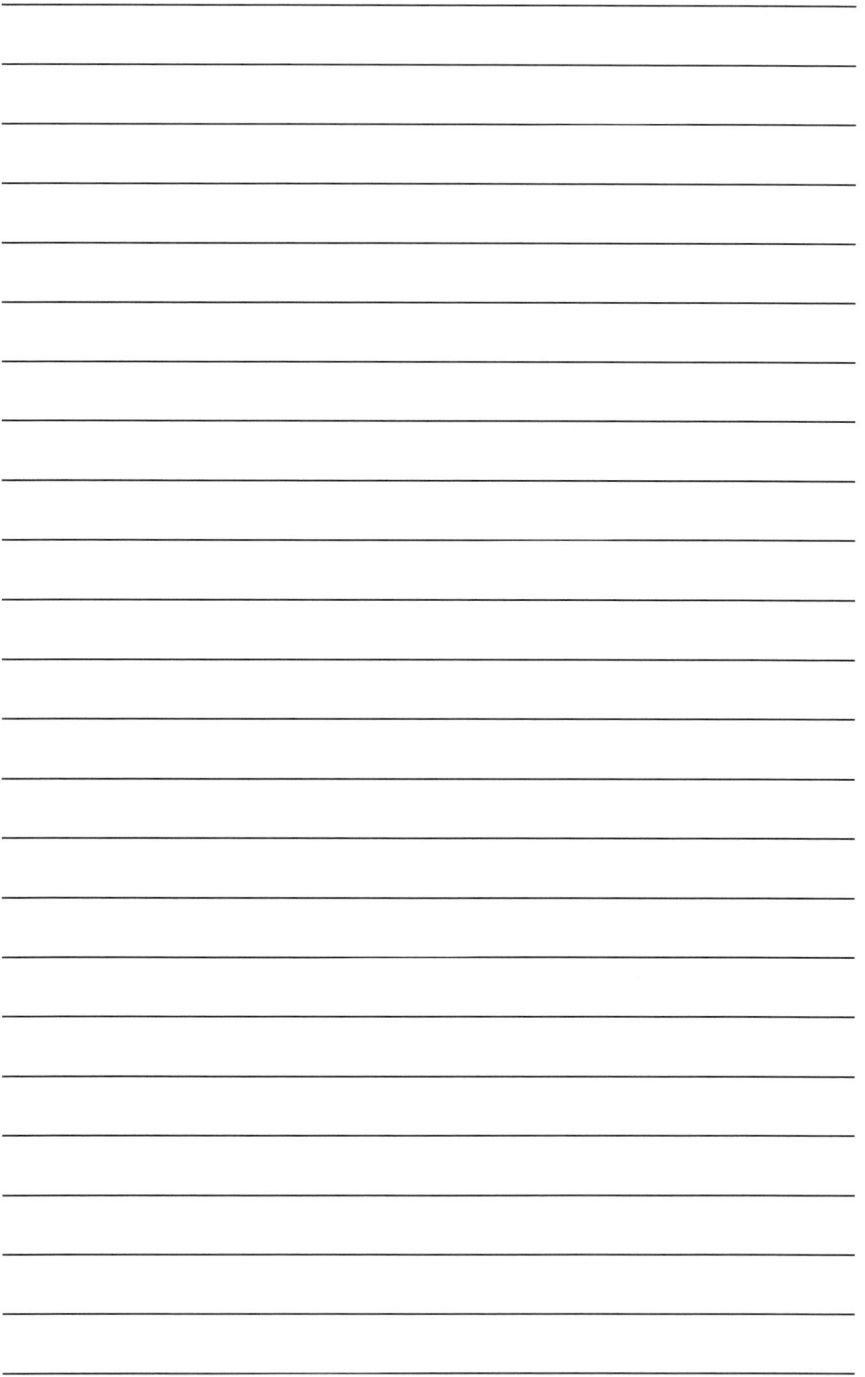

Very truly I tell you, whoever believes in me will do the works I have been doing, and they will do even greater things than these, because I am going to the Father.
John 14:12-14

Count to 3 as you take a deep breath in and let it out slowly as you count to 7. Sit quietly. Do you see or hear anything? Write your thoughts on the following pages.

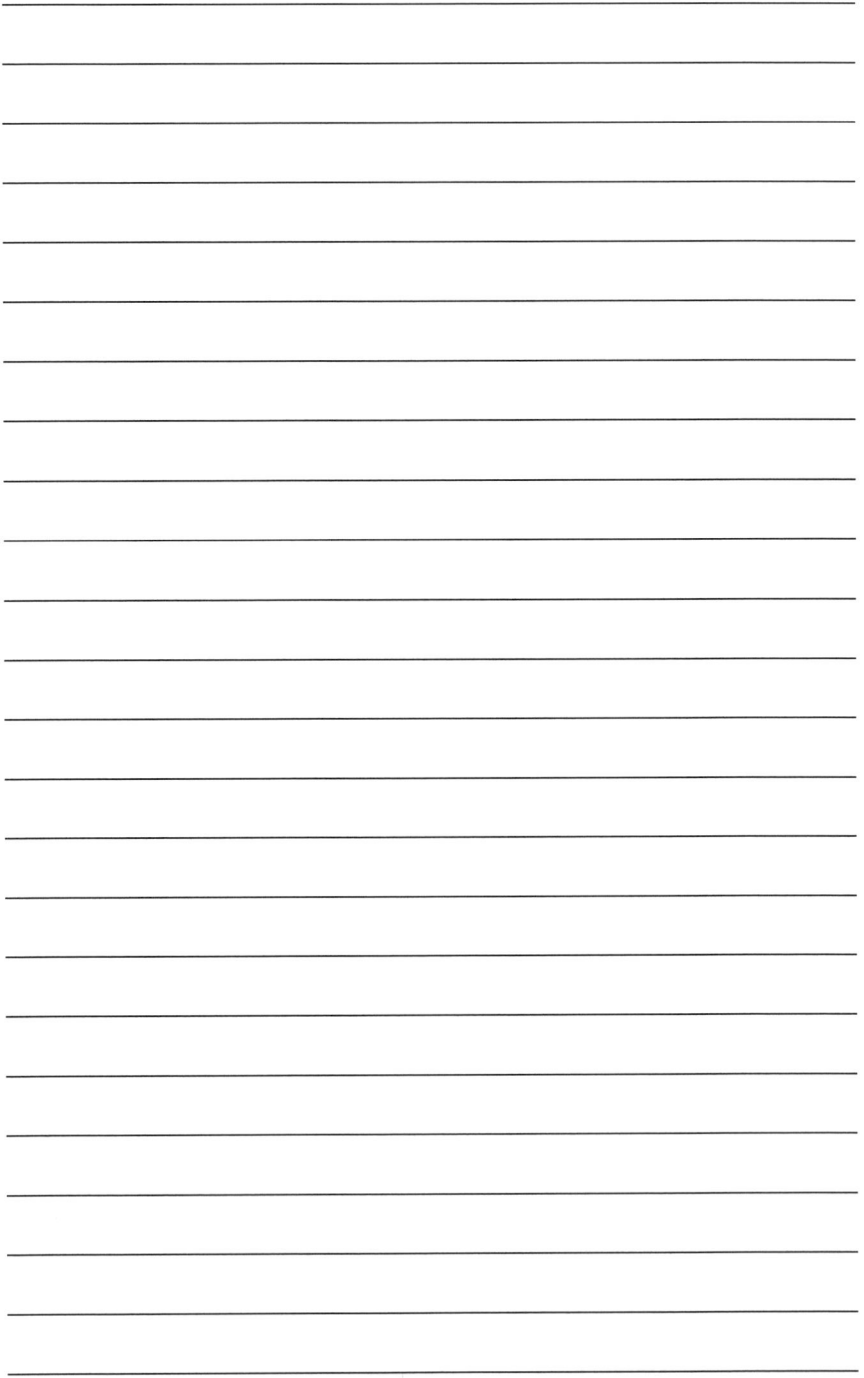

For rebellion is like the sin of divination, and arrogance like the evil of idolatry. Because you have rejected the word of the LORD, he has rejected you as king.
1 Samuel 15:23

Count to 3 as you take a deep breath in and let it out slowly as you count to 7. Sit quietly. Do you see or hear anything? Write your thoughts on the following pages.

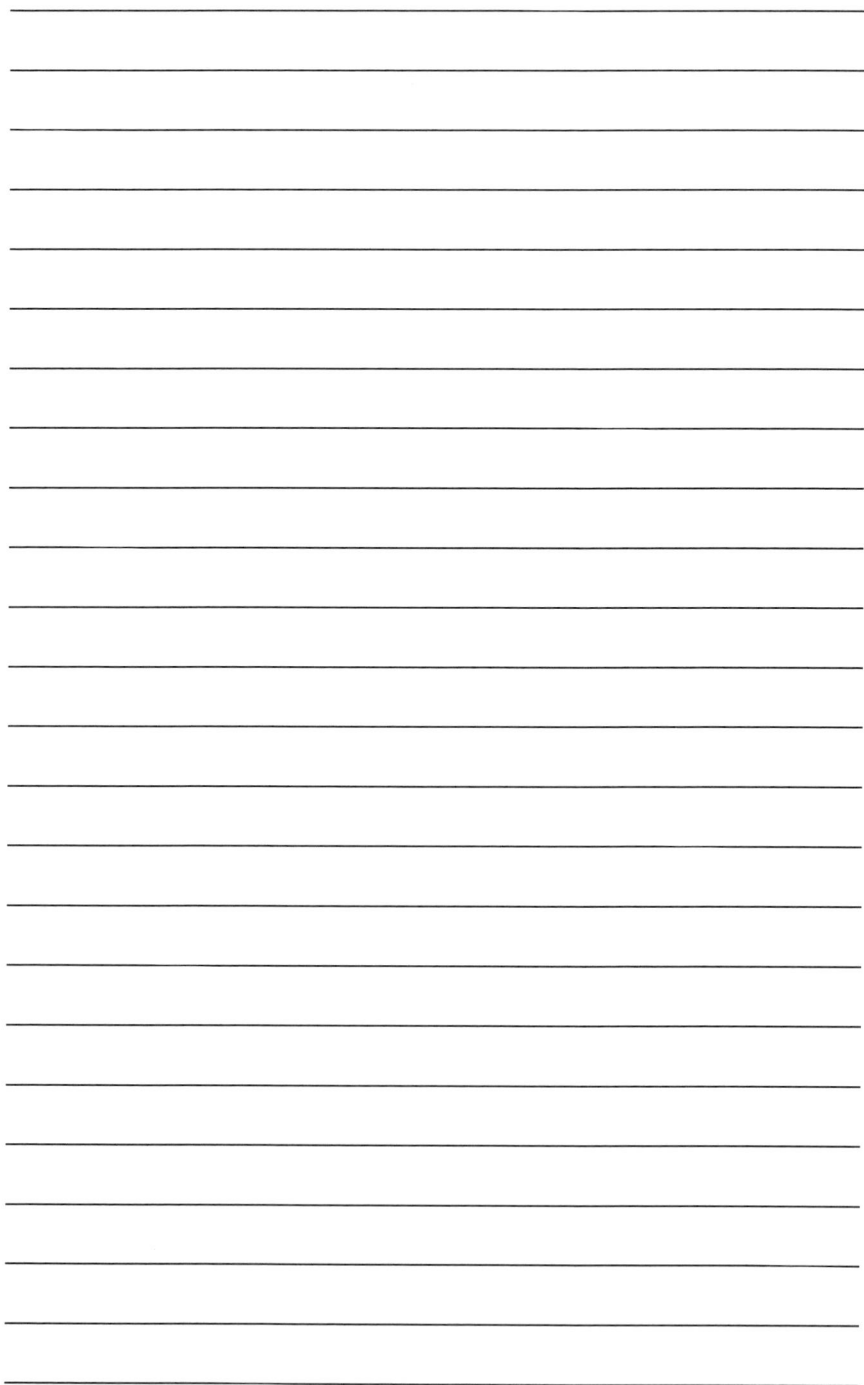

And that you be renewed in the spirit of your mind, and put on the new self, which in the likeness of God has been created in righteousness and holiness of the truth.
Ephesians 4:23-24

Count to 3 as you take a deep breath in and let it out slowly as you count to 7. Sit quietly. Do you see or hear anything? Write your thoughts on the following pages.

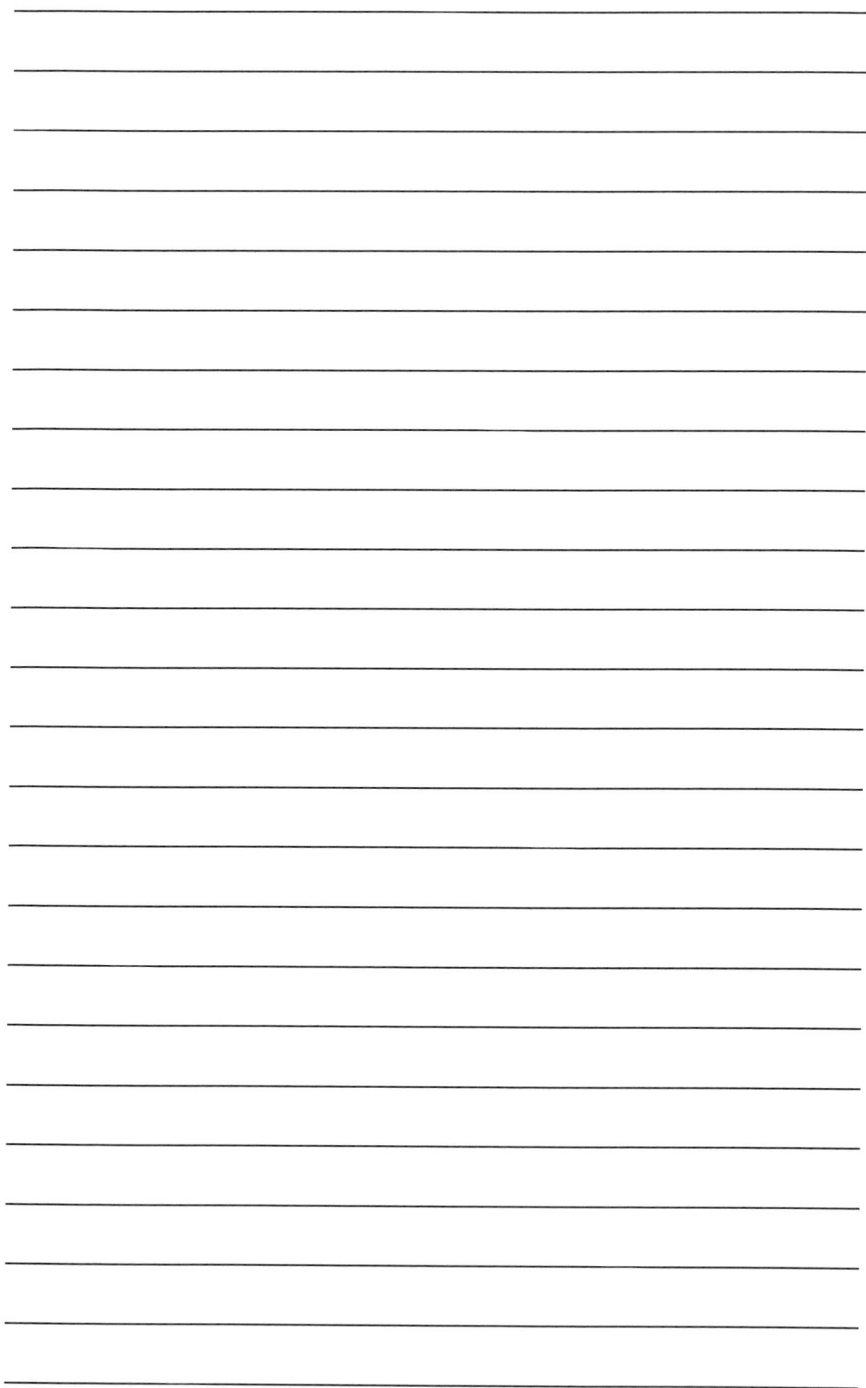

Heal the sick who are there and tell them, 'The kingdom of God has come near to you.'
Luke 10:9

Count to 3 as you take a deep breath in and let it out slowly as you count to 7. Sit quietly. Do you see or hear anything? Write your thoughts on the following pages.

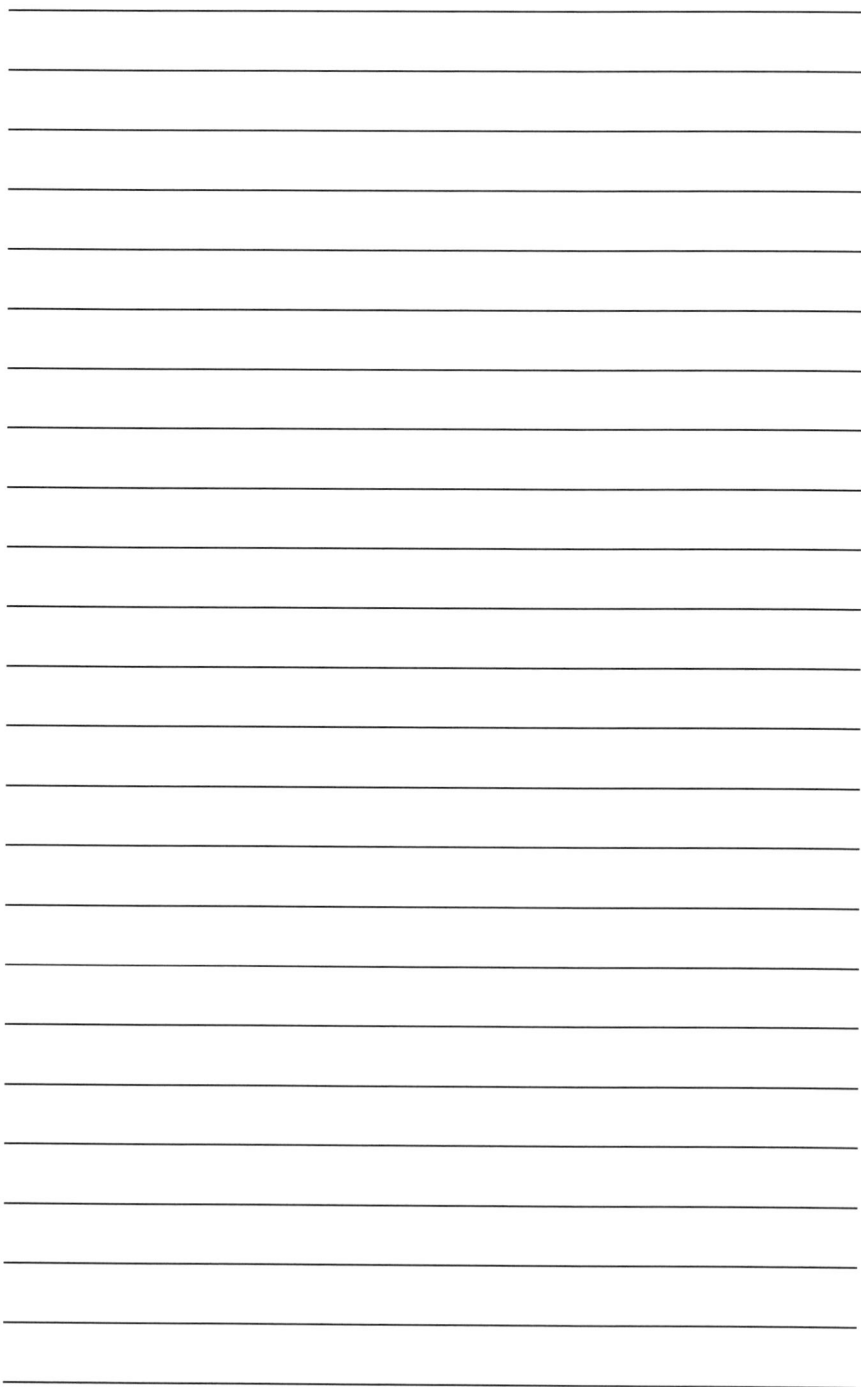

Hearing the Voice of God

Dear Lord,

Thank you for the secret place; the place where I can meet you. This is where I want to abide, in a place where you cover me with your feathers.

Lord I want nothing but to sit in your presence and hear your voice

Holy Spirit, Right now, I ask that you quiet my mind. I give you full authority over me. I surrender and receive you now, in Jesus name.

Speak Lord,
Your servant is listening....

Whoever dwells in the shelter of the Most High will rest in the shadow of the Almighty.
Psalm 91:1

Count to 3 as you take a deep breath in and let it out slowly as you count to 7. Sit quietly. Do you see or hear anything? Write your thoughts on the following pages.

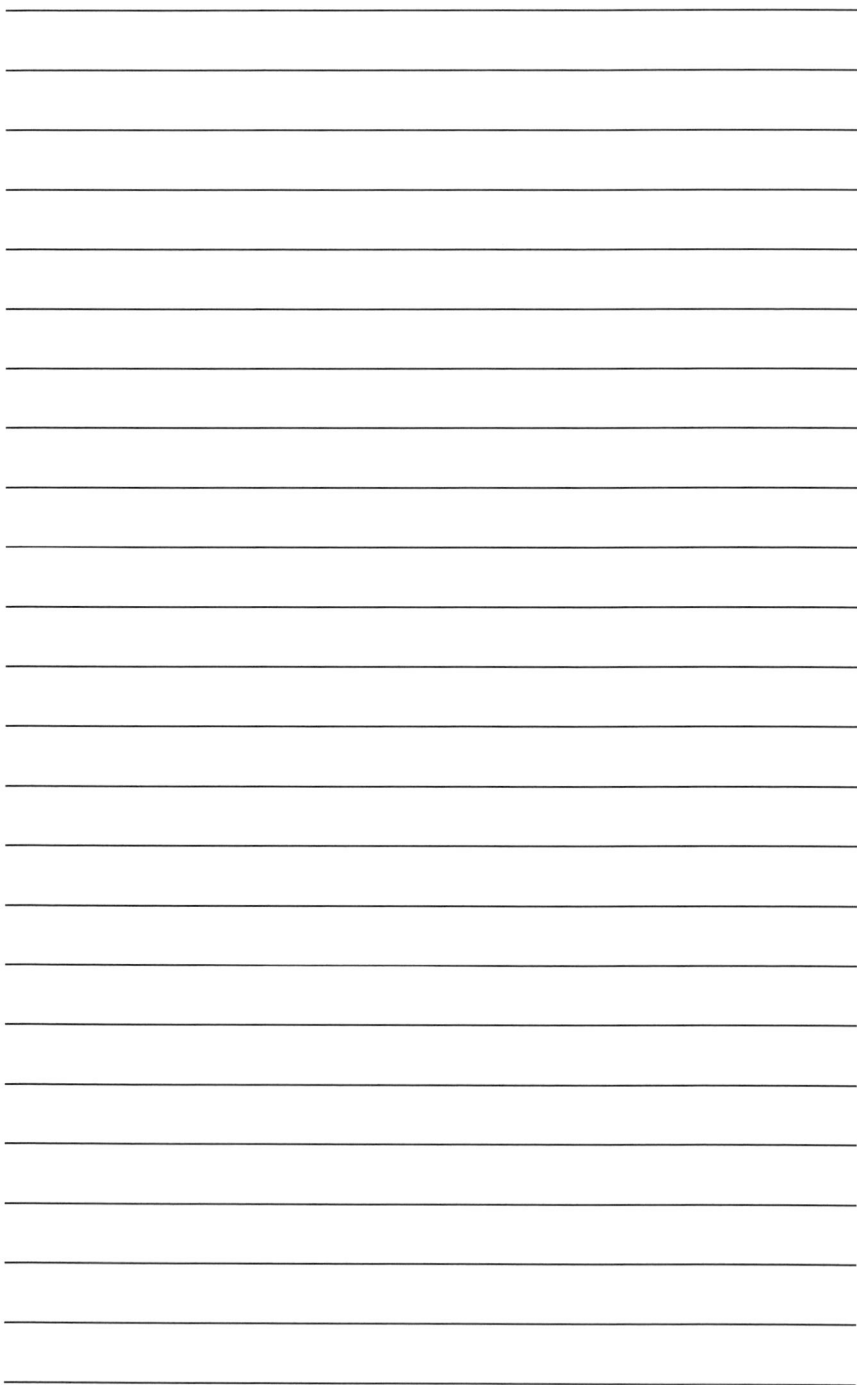

He will cover you with his feathers, and under his wings you will find refuge;
his faithfulness will be your shield and rampart.
Psalm 91:4

Count to 3 as you take a deep breath in and let it out slowly as you count to 7. Sit quietly. Do you see or hear anything? Write your thoughts on the following pages.

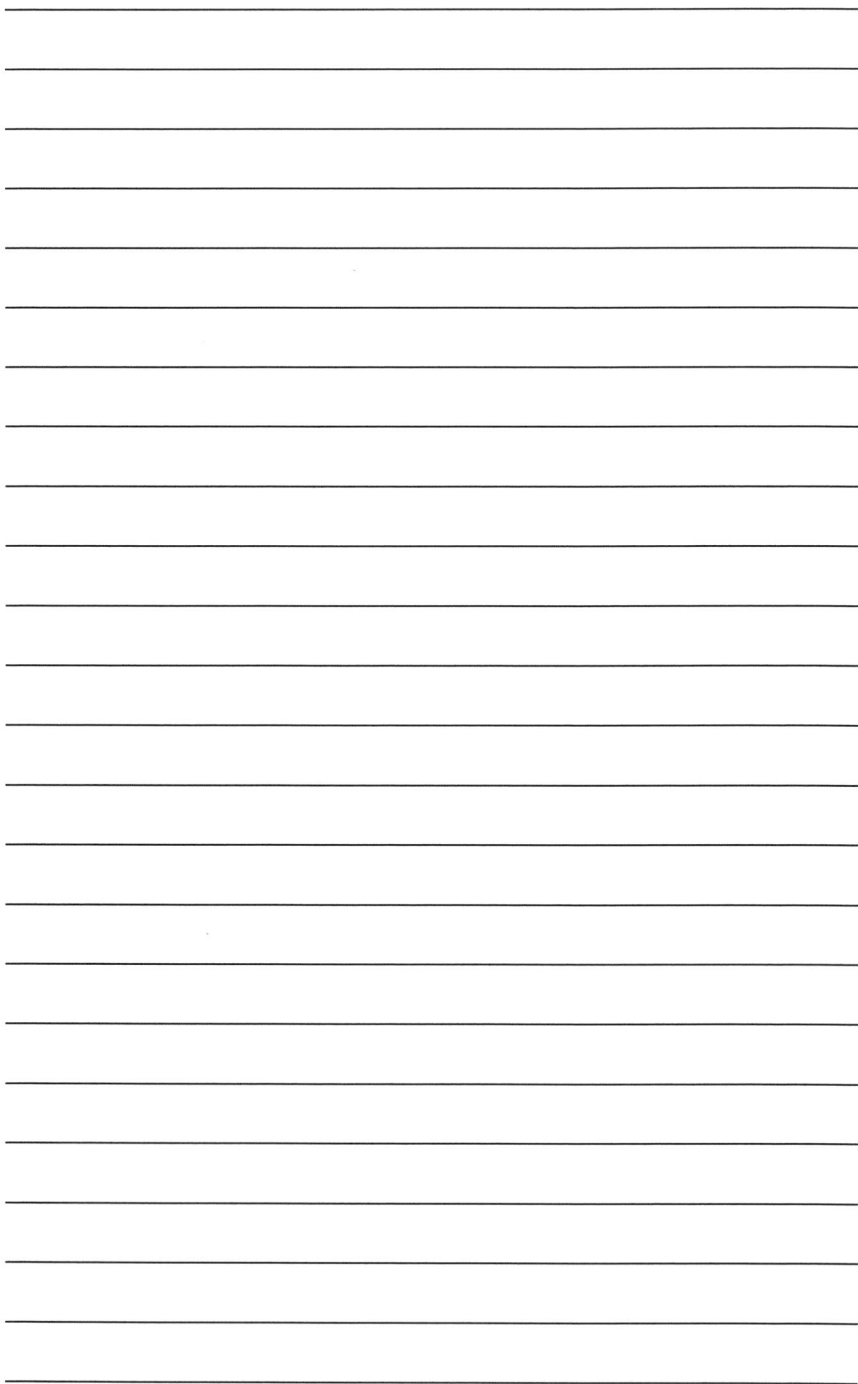

The LORD came and stood there, calling as at the other times, "Samuel! Samuel!" Then Samuel said, "Speak, for your servant is listening."
1 Samuel 3:10

Count to 3 as you take a deep breath in and let it out slowly as you count to 7. Sit quietly. Do you see or hear anything? Write your thoughts on the following pages.

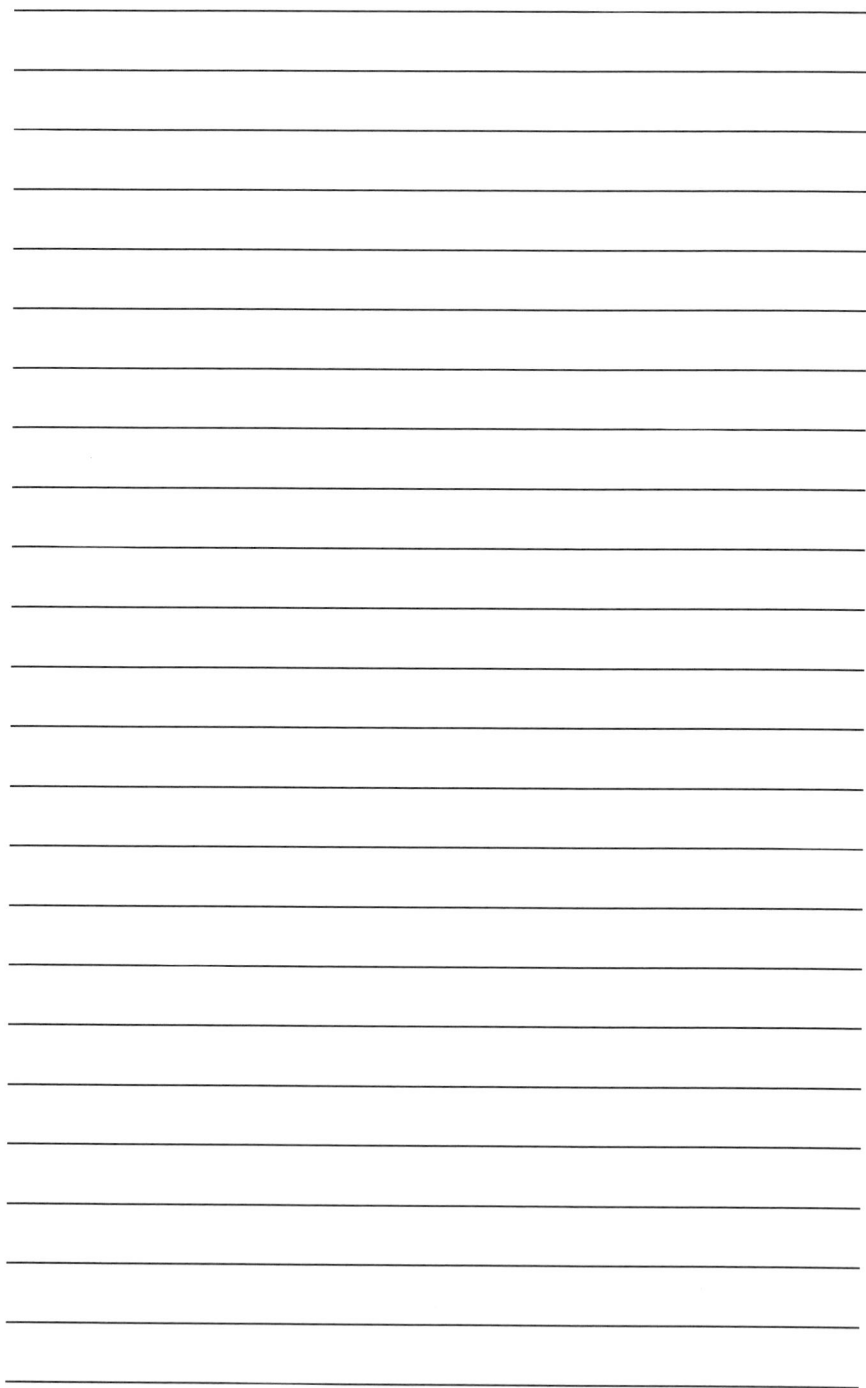

Intercede

Lord,

Thank you for who you are. Thank you for your gentle kindness, your faithfulness and your love. I am in awe of you.
I want to let go of all my cares. I cast them unto you because you care for me.
I want to allow you to use me to intercede in prayer, Father.
My spirit is yearning to be used by you.
My spirit is crying out to you as you cry out to me. Deep is calling unto deep. Father, as the deer pants for the water, so my soul longs after you.
I want nothing tangible.
I want what my eyes can't see.
I want your glory.
I want the things you want.
Your desire is that we speak encouraging words to one another and that no one is left behind. You said that it is good for us to intercede in prayer.
Lord, you'll leave the 99 for the 1.
Lord, by your Spirit, who do you want me to pray for? Who do you want me to war for, spiritually? Who or what do you need me to speak life over? I'm ready, open, willing and I'll be obedient. Not my will but yours Father.

In Jesus name I pray, Amen.

Cast all your anxiety on him because he cares for you
1 Peter 5:7

Count to 3 as you take a deep breath in and let it out slowly as you count to 7. Sit quietly. Do you see or hear anything? Write your thoughts on the following pages.

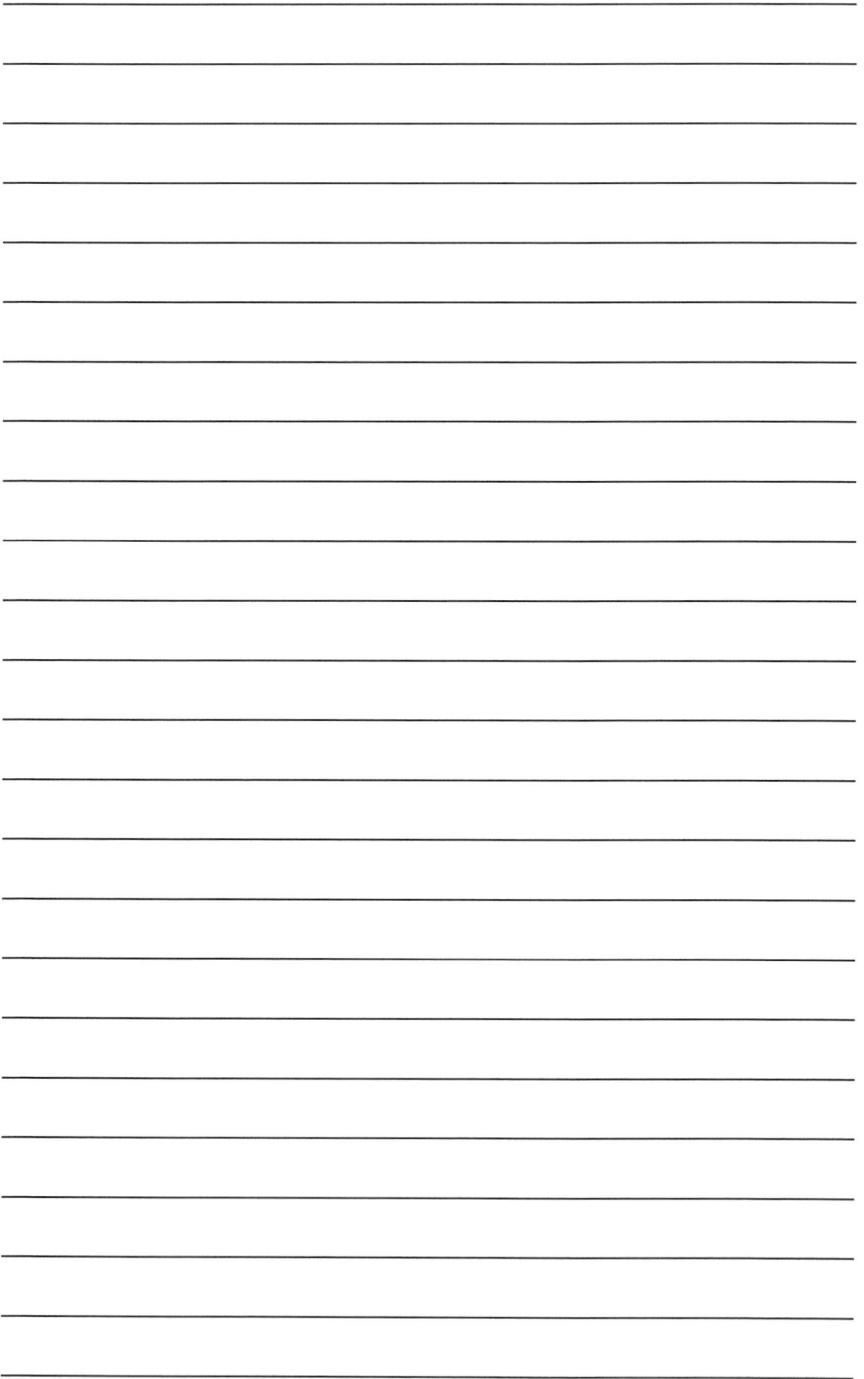

My soul thirsts for God, for the living God. When can I go and meet with God?
Psalm 42:1-2

Count to 3 as you take a deep breath in and let it out slowly as you count to 7. Sit quietly. Do you see or hear anything? Write your thoughts on the following pages.

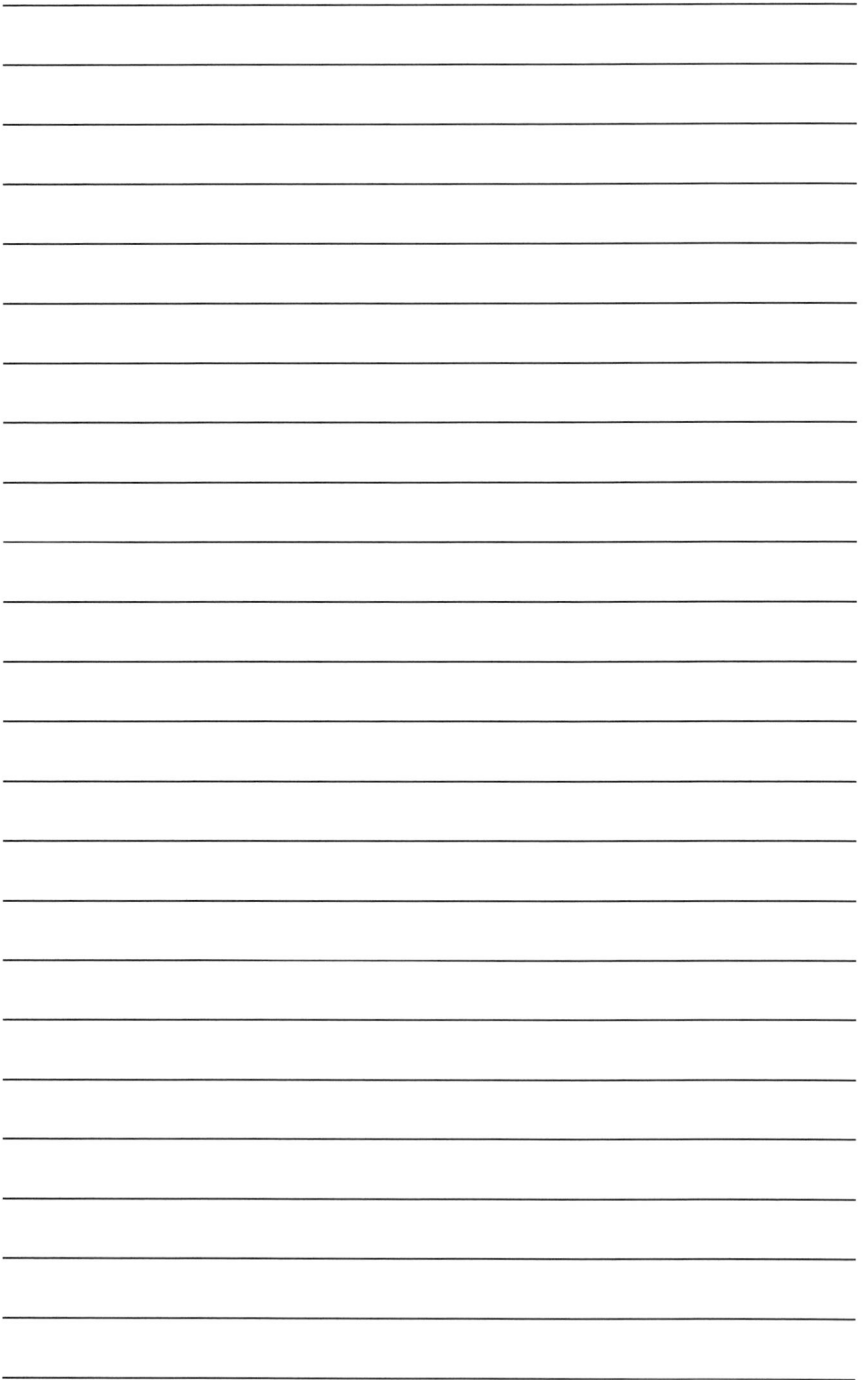

Deep calls to deep in the roar of your waterfalls; all your waves and breakers have swept over me.
Psalm 42:7

Count to 3 as you take a deep breath in and let it out slowly as you count to 7. Sit quietly. Do you see or hear anything? Write your thoughts on the following pages.

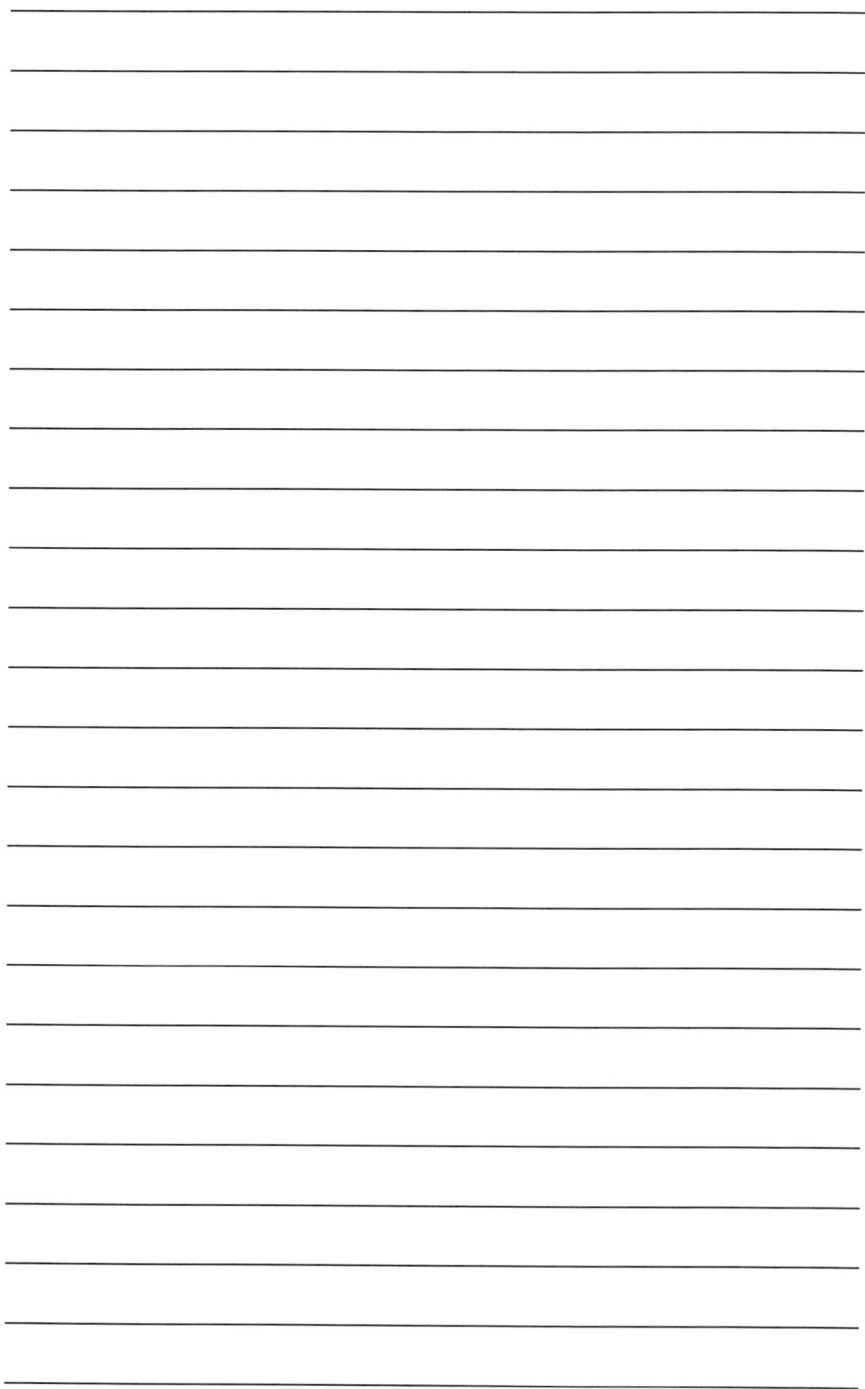

"What do you think? If a man owns a hundred sheep, and one of them wanders away, will he not leave the ninety-nine on the hills and go to look for the one that wandered off?
Matthew 18:12

Count to 3 as you take a deep breath in and let it out slowly as you count to 7. Sit quietly. Do you see or hear anything? Write your thoughts on the following pages.

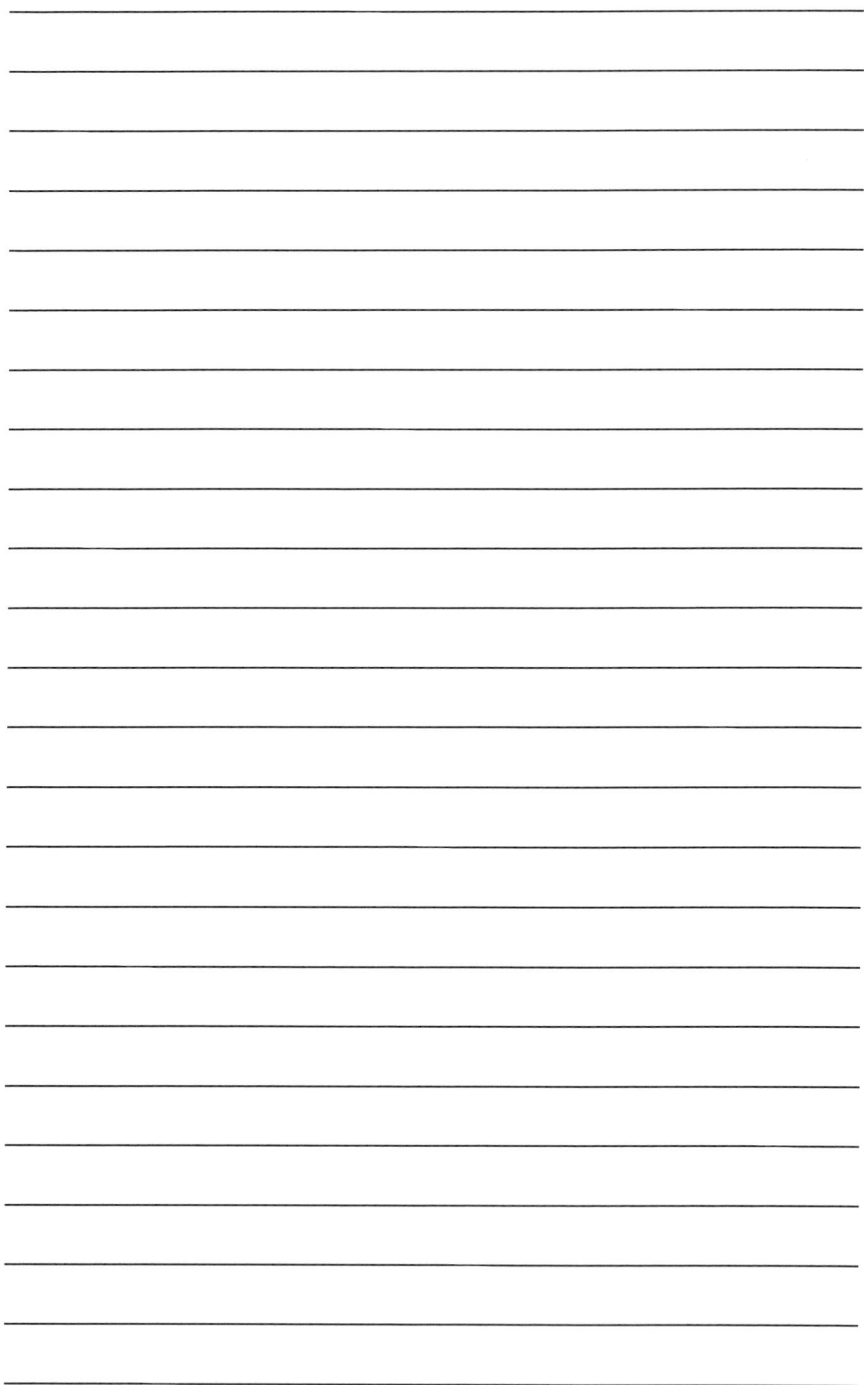

Therefore encourage one another and build each other up, just as in fact you are doing
1 Thessalonians 5:11

Count to 3 as you take a deep breath in and let it out slowly as you count to 7. Sit quietly. Do you see or hear anything? Write your thoughts on the following pages.

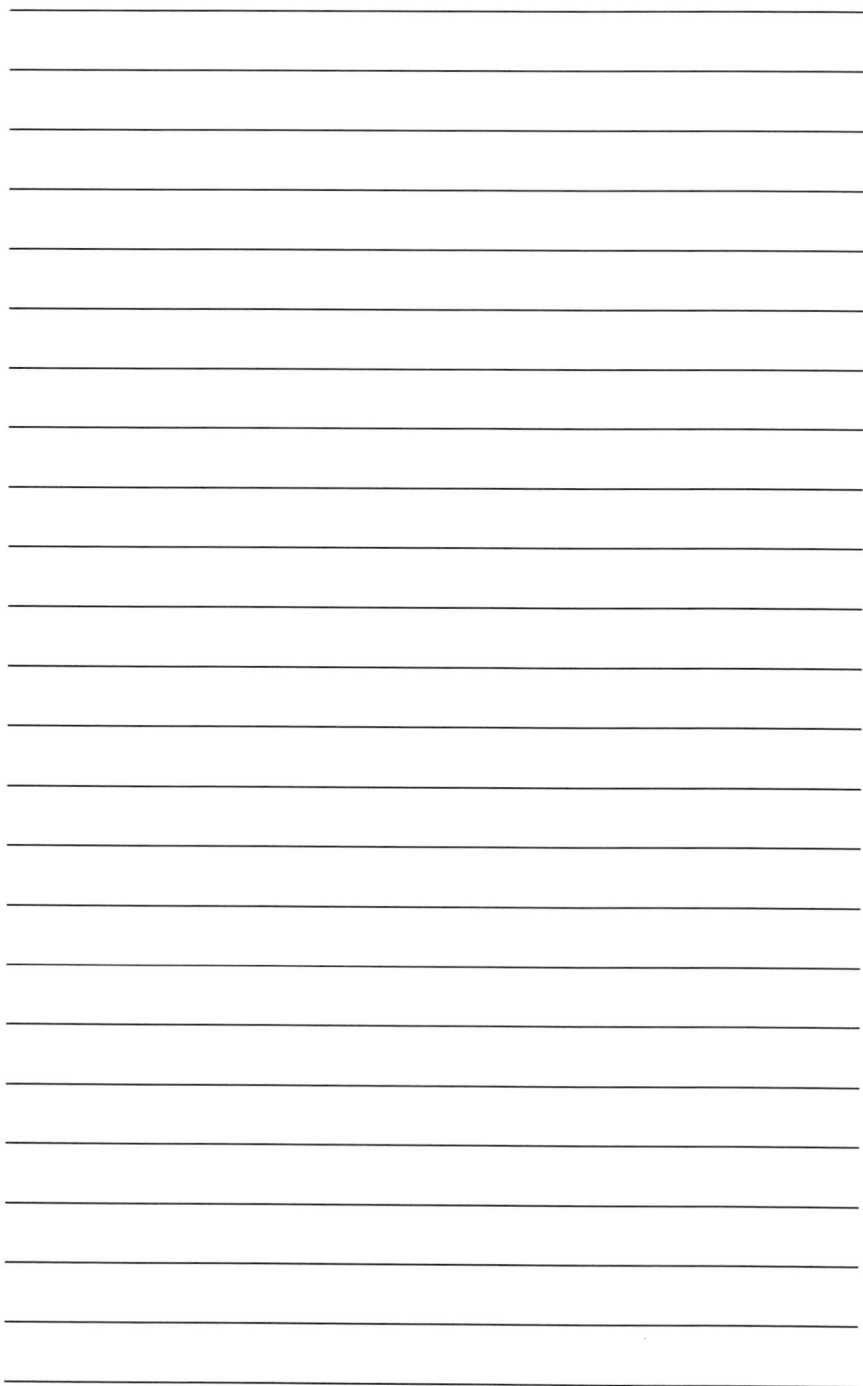

I urge, then, first of all, that petitions, prayers, intercession and thanksgiving be made for all people-
1 Timothy 2:1

Count to 3 as you take a deep breath in and let it out slowly as you count to 7. Sit quietly. Do you see or hear anything? Write your thoughts on the following pages.

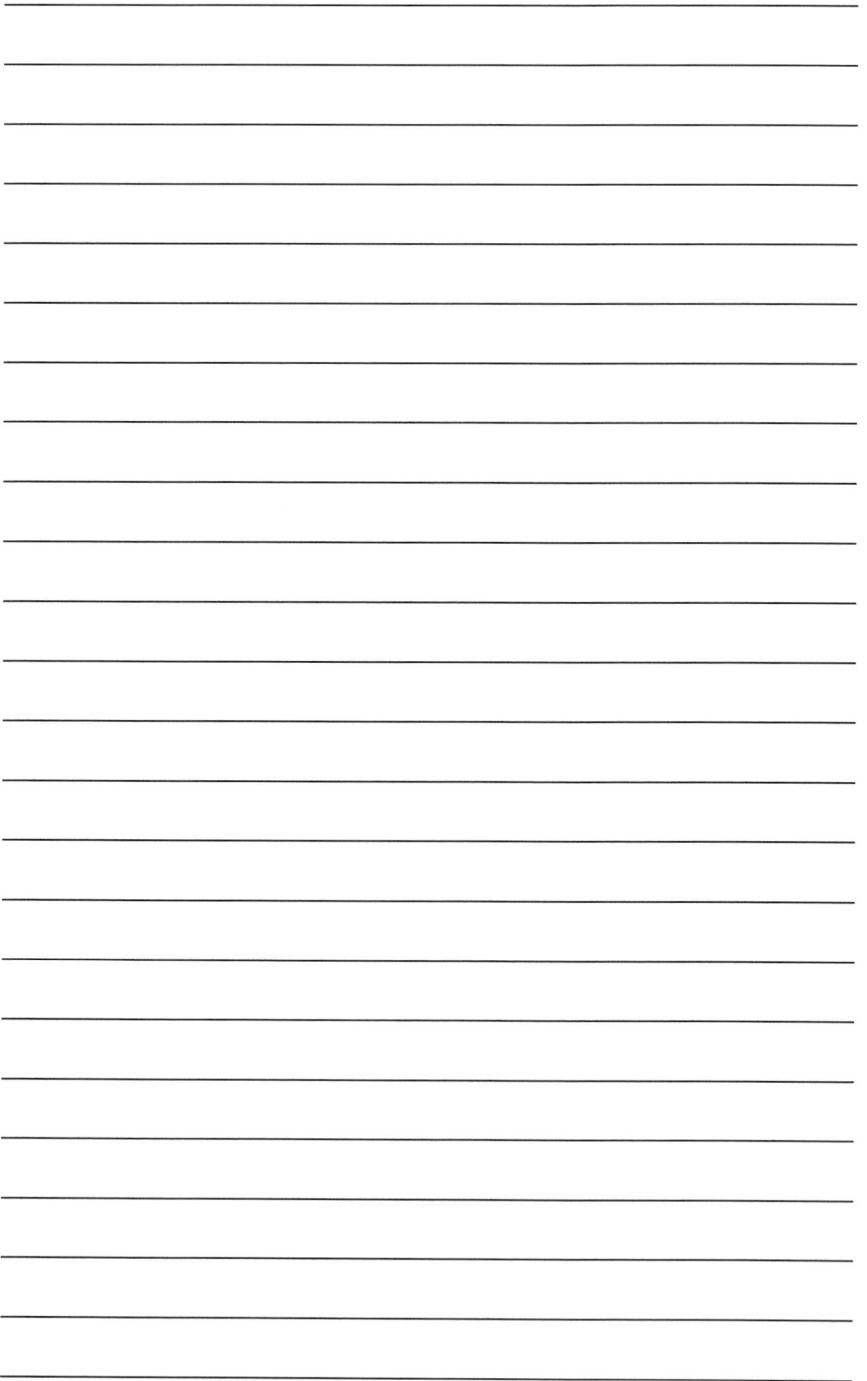

Go Deeper

Lord,

Thank you for this gift of life.
Thank you, Lord that you knew me from before I was in my mothers' womb.
Thank you that you chose me. You called me and you make no mistakes. You are not a man that you should lie. You said I'm holy, I'm righteous and I'm set apart. You called me peculiar.
It's so hard to understand your wonderful ways.
Lord, I want to understand your mysteries.
I want to know you more.
I desire to understand who I am in Christ.
I desire to understand more.
You told me to delight in you and you will give me my hearts desires.
I desire to see as you see.
I desire to love the way you love.
I desire to accept the way you accept.
I desire to not be double minded and question you but partner with you as I fulfill my assignment here.
I desire to surrender. I do surrender.
I just want you. I desire more of you. But if I cannot handle it right now, I desire to receive you more in how you have revealed yourself to me already.
I just desire you.
I love you. And it is so hard to understand this love. I question you but I come to you.
I desire to no longer be carnal in my actions, but to be spiritual.
I desire to give you all the glory. I want you to use my life in a way that all men will seek you because of what you have done in my life.

God, your word says if I ask, I will receive. Your word says if I seek, I will find. Your word says if I knock, the doors will be opened. I'm asking you to give me my hearts desires. I'm asking that you activate your Holy Spirit in me to seek you fervently like never before. I cannot do it on my own. Only by your Spirit can I do it, not by might nor by power. I am knocking Father, would you please open the door?

I ask this all In Jesus' mighty name. My cornerstone, my prince of peace, my wonderful counselor, my savior. Would you help me understand that as well? Jesus being the savior of the world? I know, my spirit and soul knows it. No matter how much I question, I'm at your feet. That in itself is a witness but can you please make your Word come alive to me? Give me revelation knowledge. Give me understanding. Give me power according to your perfect will. Stir up the gifts within me. Protect me from the evil one who will try to hinder me from seeking you. Father, increase my discernment. Increase my wisdom. You said if I lack wisdom and ask for it, you will give it generously.

Father, you said your word does not return to you void but shall accomplish that in which you purposed it. Break up any fallow ground Lord, so that your word may be sowed in healthy soil and produce lasting fruit in me.

In the wonderful name of Jesus, I pray, Amen.

I praise you because I am fearfully and wonderfully made; your works are wonderful, I know that full well.
Psalm 139:14

Count to 3 as you take a deep breath in and let it out slowly as you count to 7. Sit quietly. Do you see or hear anything? Write your thoughts on the following pages.

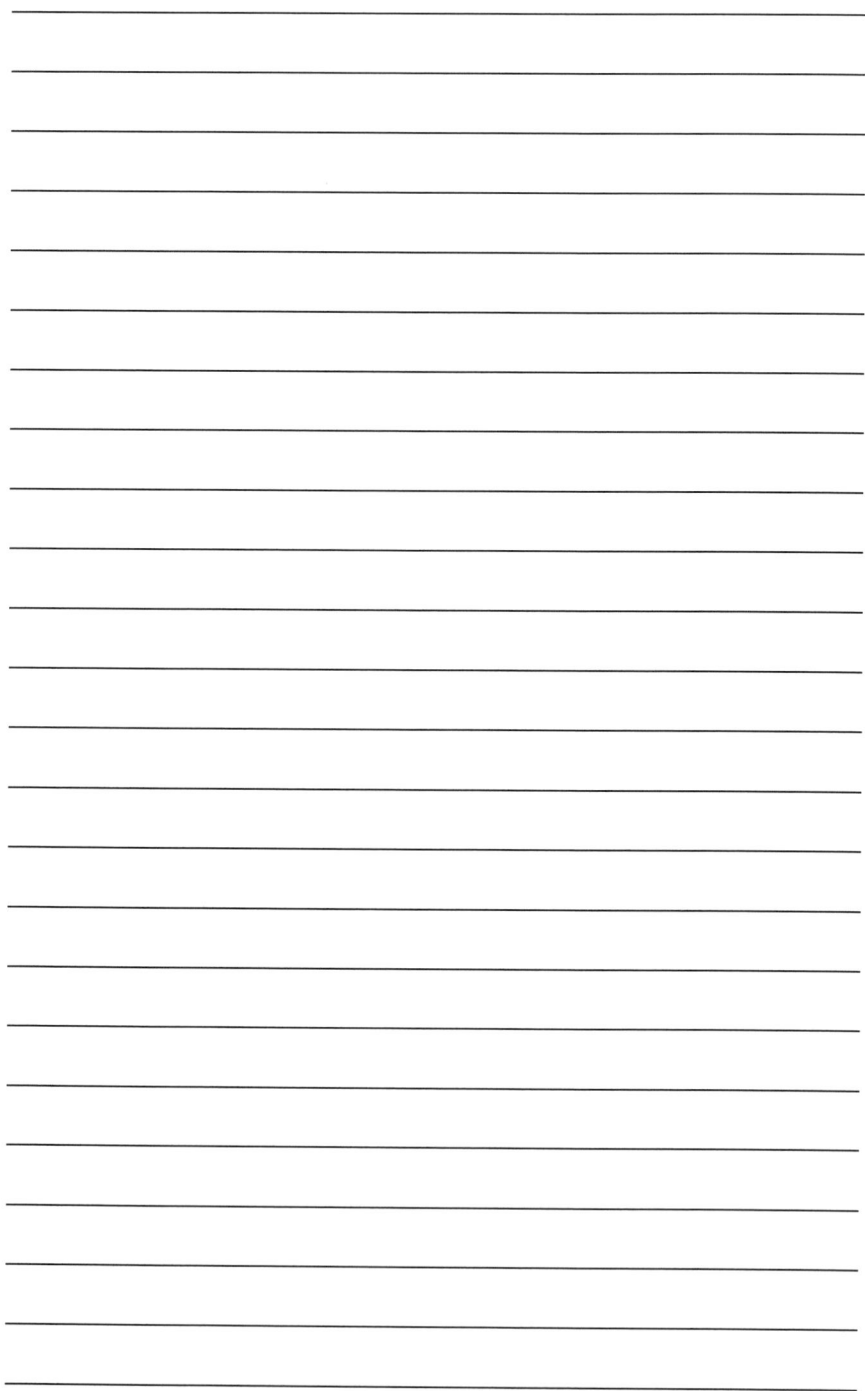

"Before I formed you in the womb I knew you, before you were born I set you apart; I appointed you as a prophet to the nations."
Jeremiah 1:5

Count to 3 as you take a deep breath in and let it out slowly as you count to 7. Sit quietly. Do you see or hear anything? Write your thoughts on the following pages.

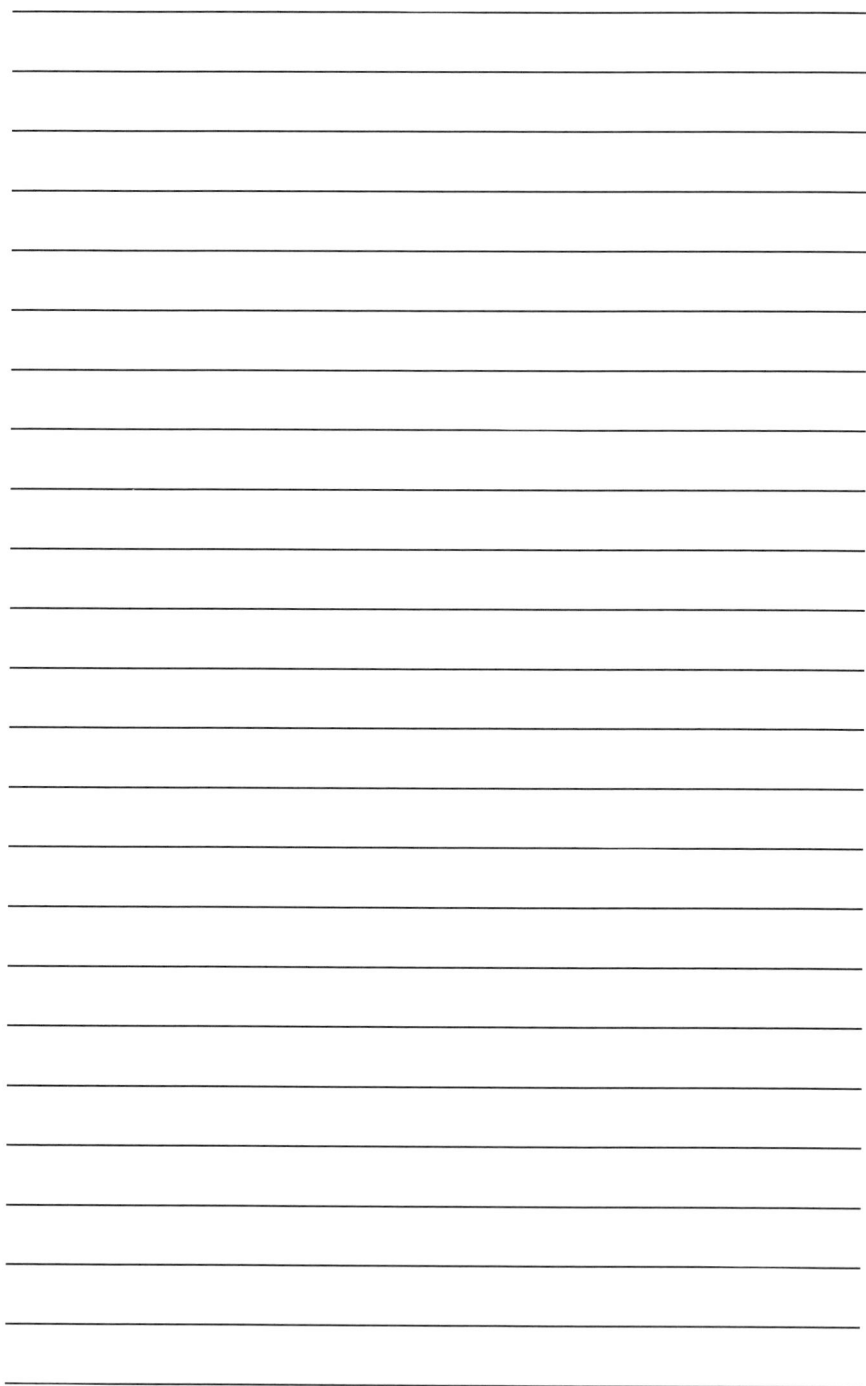

But you are a chosen people, a royal priesthood, a holy nation, God's special possession, that you may declare the praises of him who called you out of darkness into his wonderful light.
1 Peter 2:9

Count to 3 as you take a deep breath in and let it out slowly as you count to 7. Sit quietly. Do you see or hear anything? Write your thoughts on the following pages.

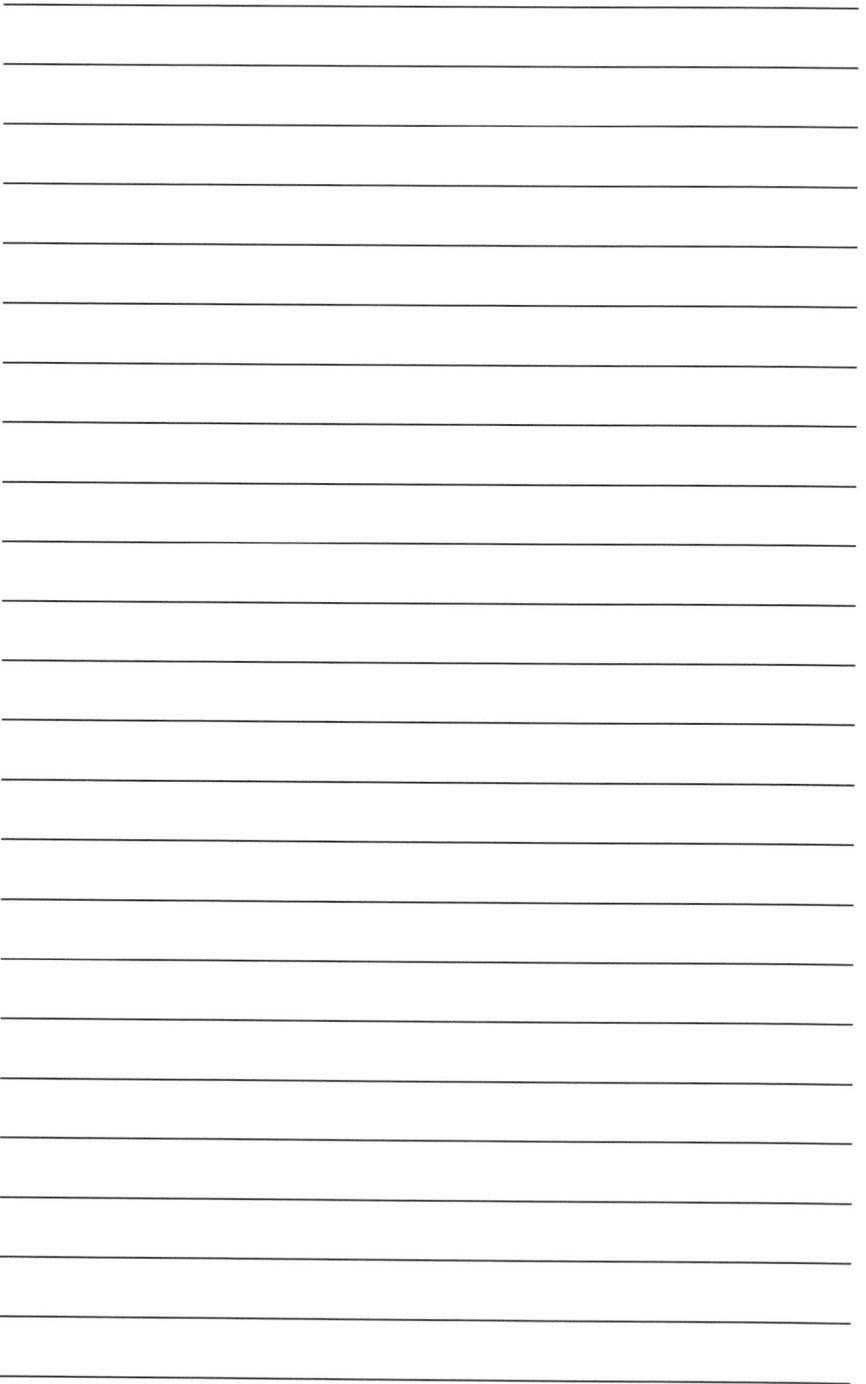

Balaam said, "Build me seven altars here, and prepare seven bulls and seven rams for me."
Numbers 23:29

Count to 3 as you take a deep breath in and let it out slowly as you count to 7. Sit quietly. Do you see or hear anything? Write your thoughts on the following pages.

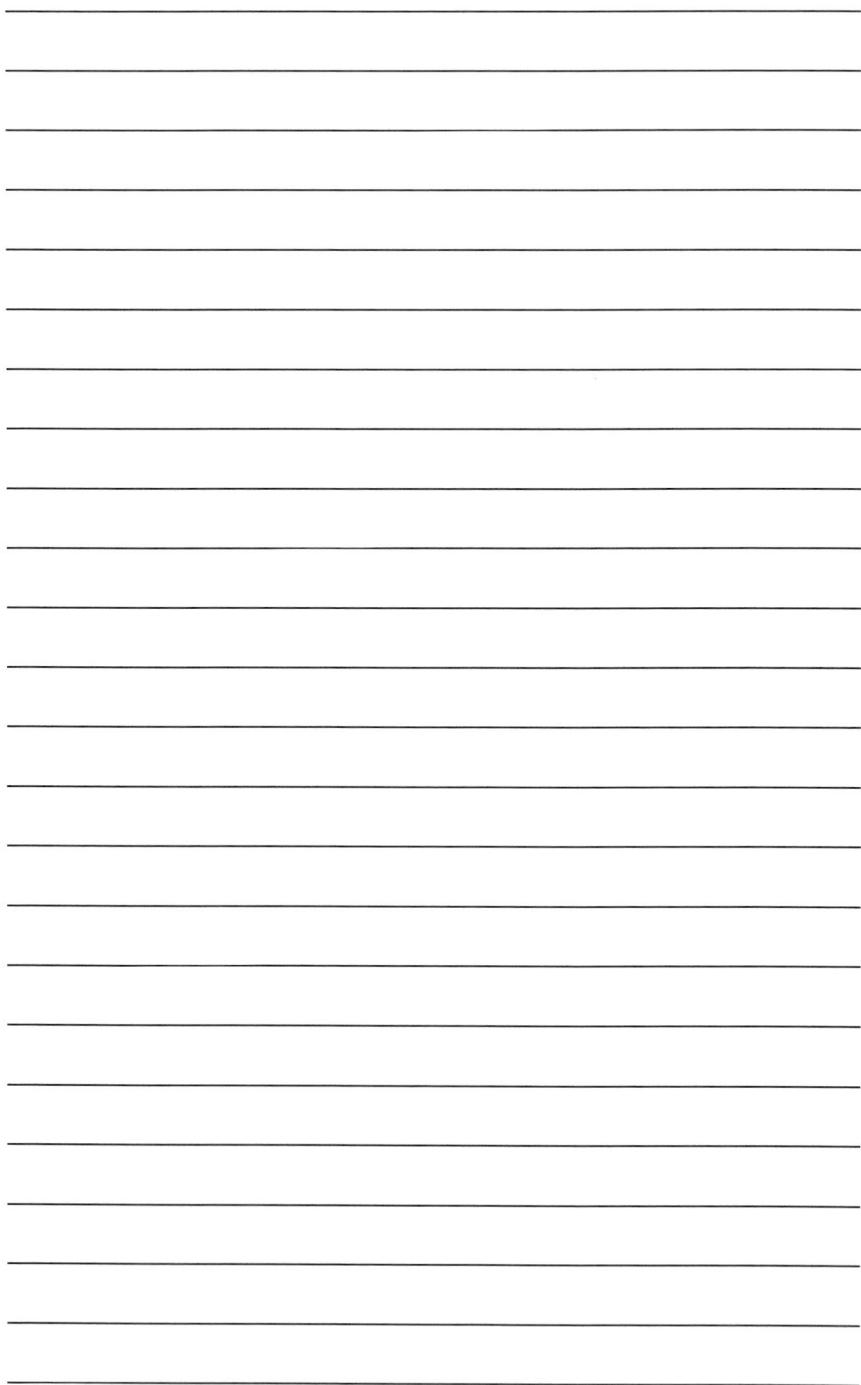

Take delight in the LORD, and he will give you the desires of your heart.
Psalm 37:4

Count to 3 as you take a deep breath in and let it out slowly as you count to 7. Sit quietly. Do you see or hear anything? Write your thoughts on the following pages.

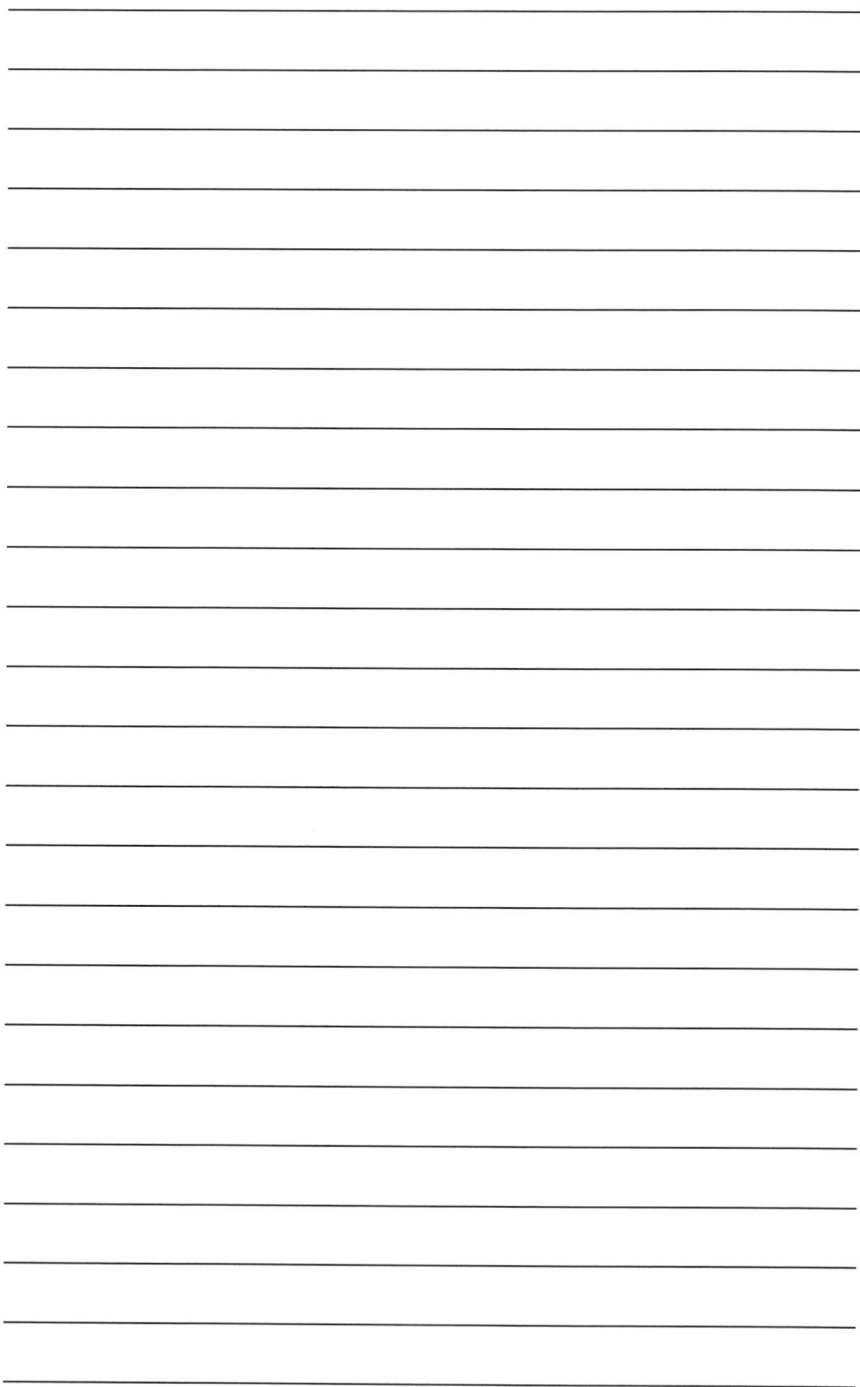

But when you ask, you must believe and not doubt, because the one who doubts is like a wave of the sea, blown and tossed by the wind.
James 1:6-8

Count to 3 as you take a deep breath in and let it out slowly as you count to 7. Sit quietly. Do you see or hear anything? Write your thoughts on the following pages.

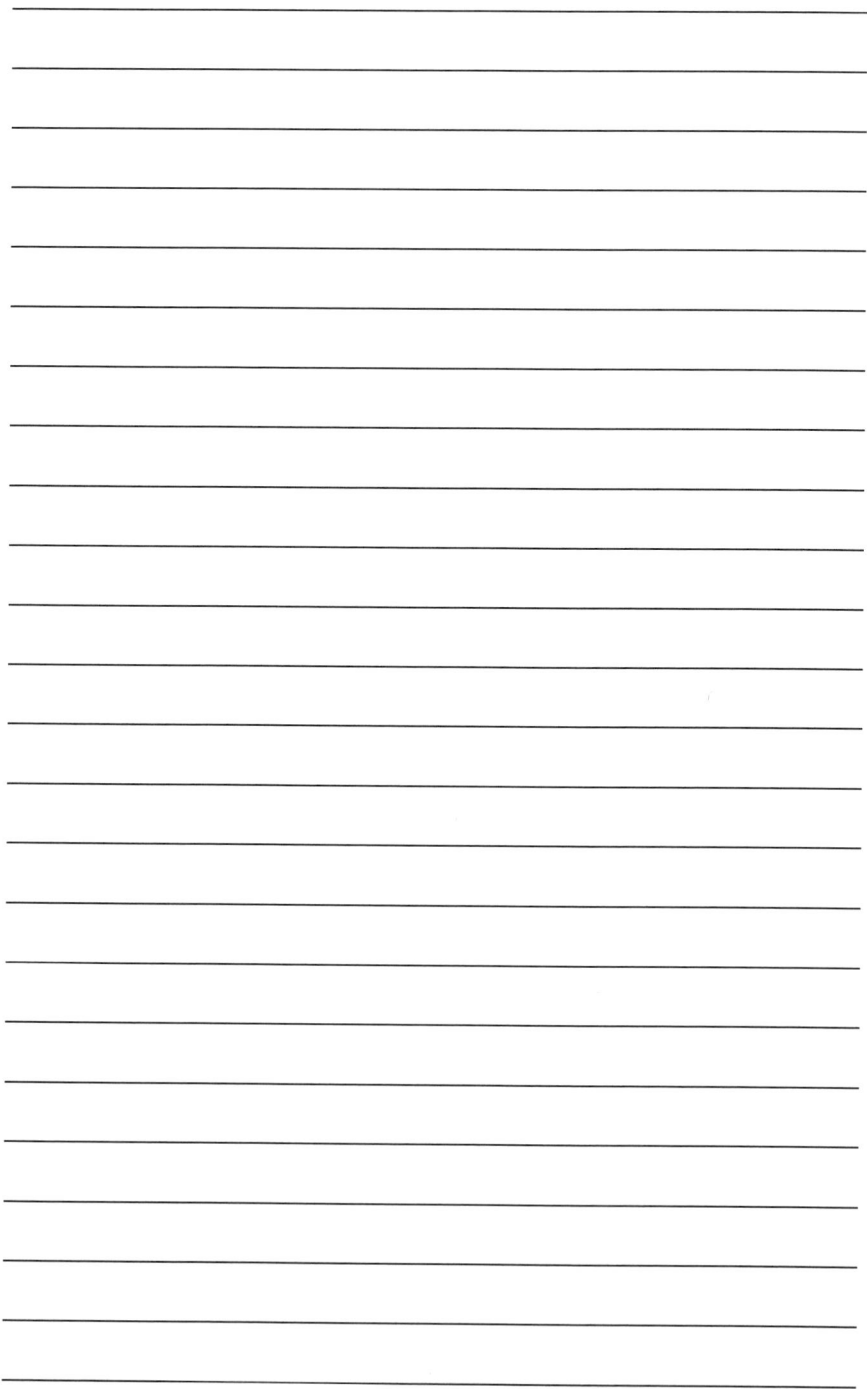

So he said to me, "This is the word of the LORD to Zerubbabel: 'Not by might nor by power, but by my Spirit,' says the LORD Almighty.
Zechariah 4:6

Count to 3 as you take a deep breath in and let it out slowly as you count to 7. Sit quietly. Do you see or hear anything? Write your thoughts on the following pages.

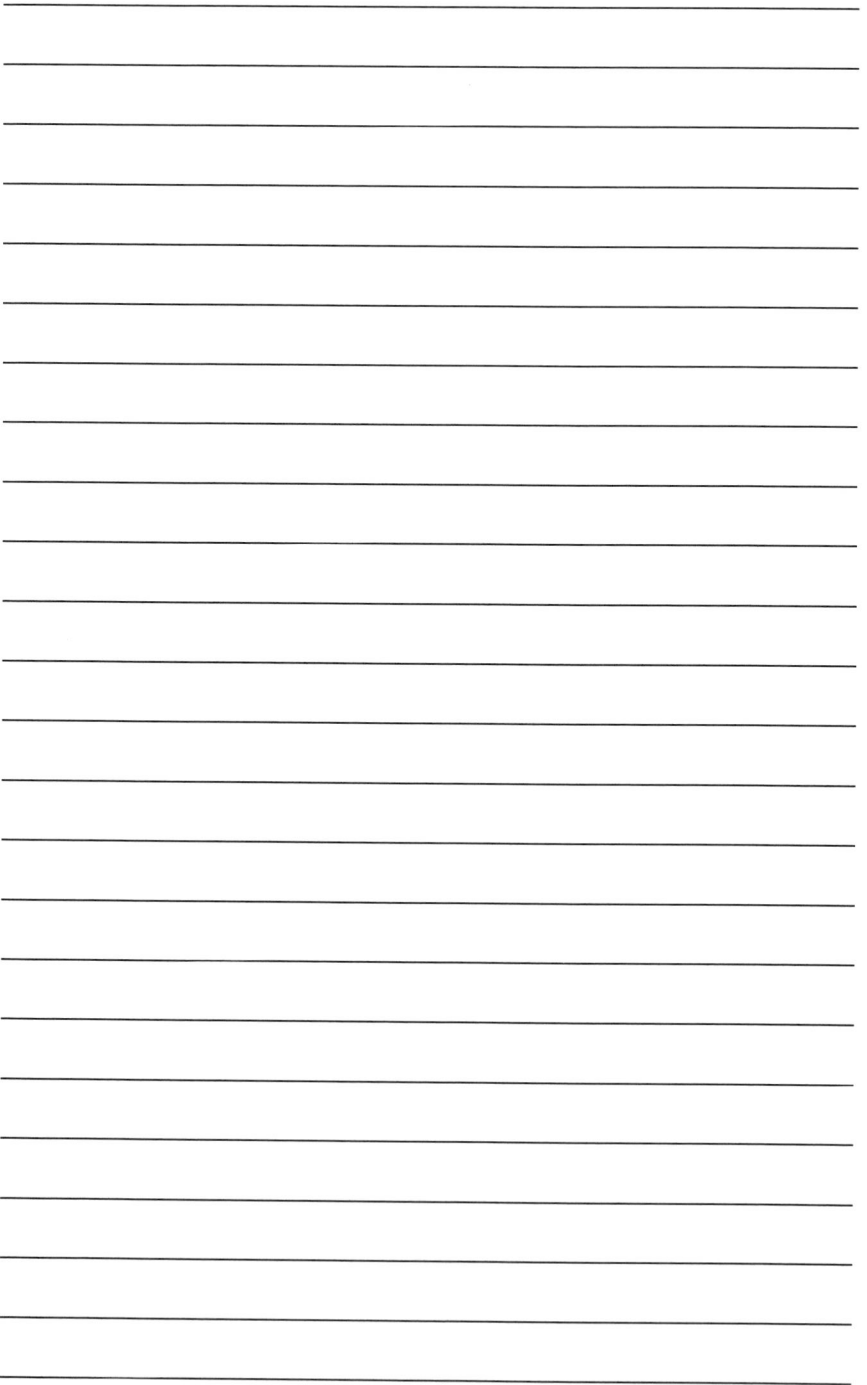

Ask and it will be given to you; seek and you will find; knock and the door will be opened to you.
Matthew 7:7

Count to 3 as you take a deep breath in and let it out slowly as you count to 7. Sit quietly. Do you see or hear anything? Write your thoughts on the following pages.

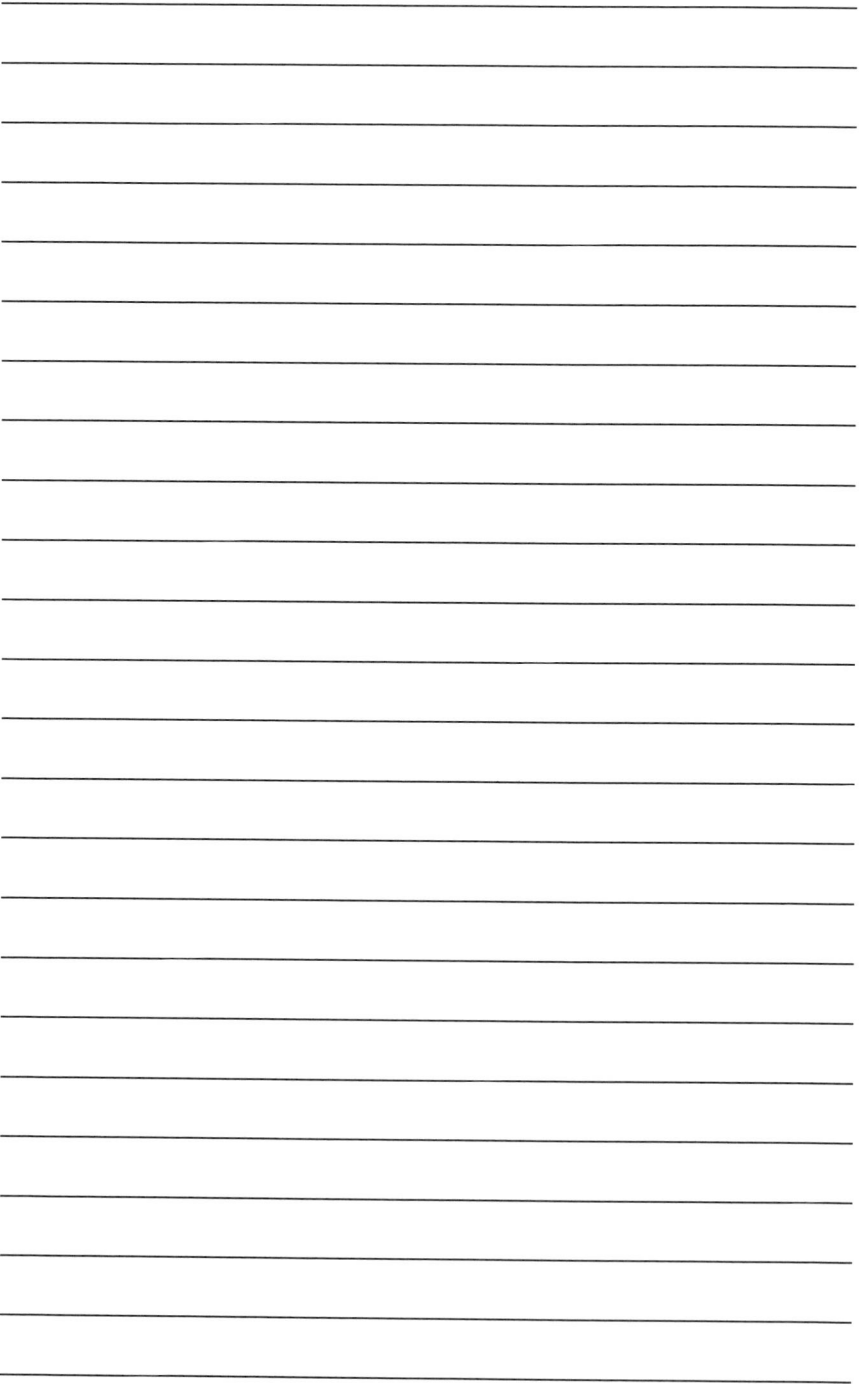

Follow the way of love and eagerly desire gifts of the Spirit, especially prophecy.
1 Corinthians 14:1

Count to 3 as you take a deep breath in and let it out slowly as you count to 7. Sit quietly. Do you see or hear anything? Write your thoughts on the following pages.

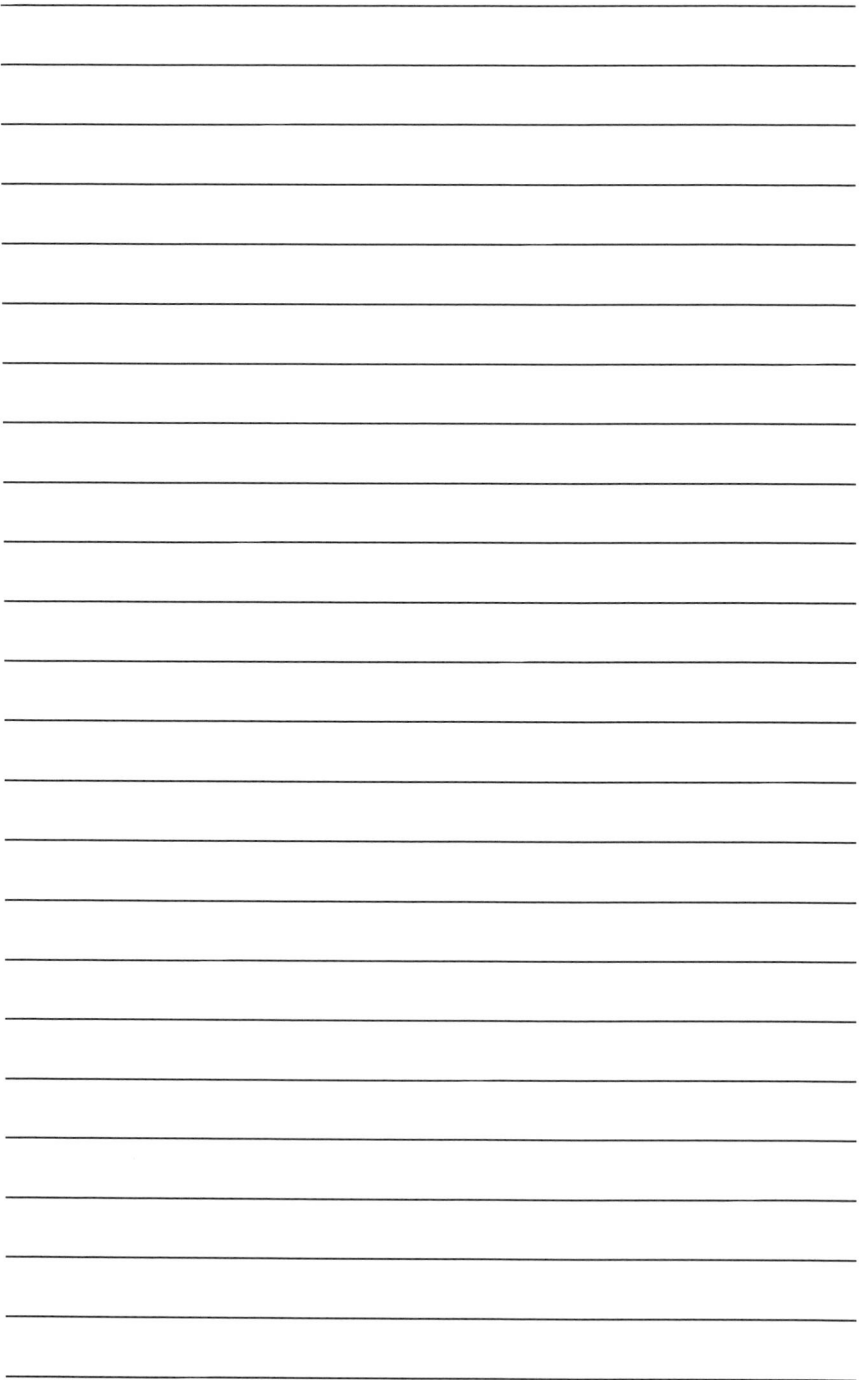

If any of you lacks wisdom, you should ask God, who gives generously to all without finding fault, and it will be given to you.
James 1:5

Count to 3 as you take a deep breath in and let it out slowly as you count to 7. Sit quietly. Do you see or hear anything? Write your thoughts on the following pages.

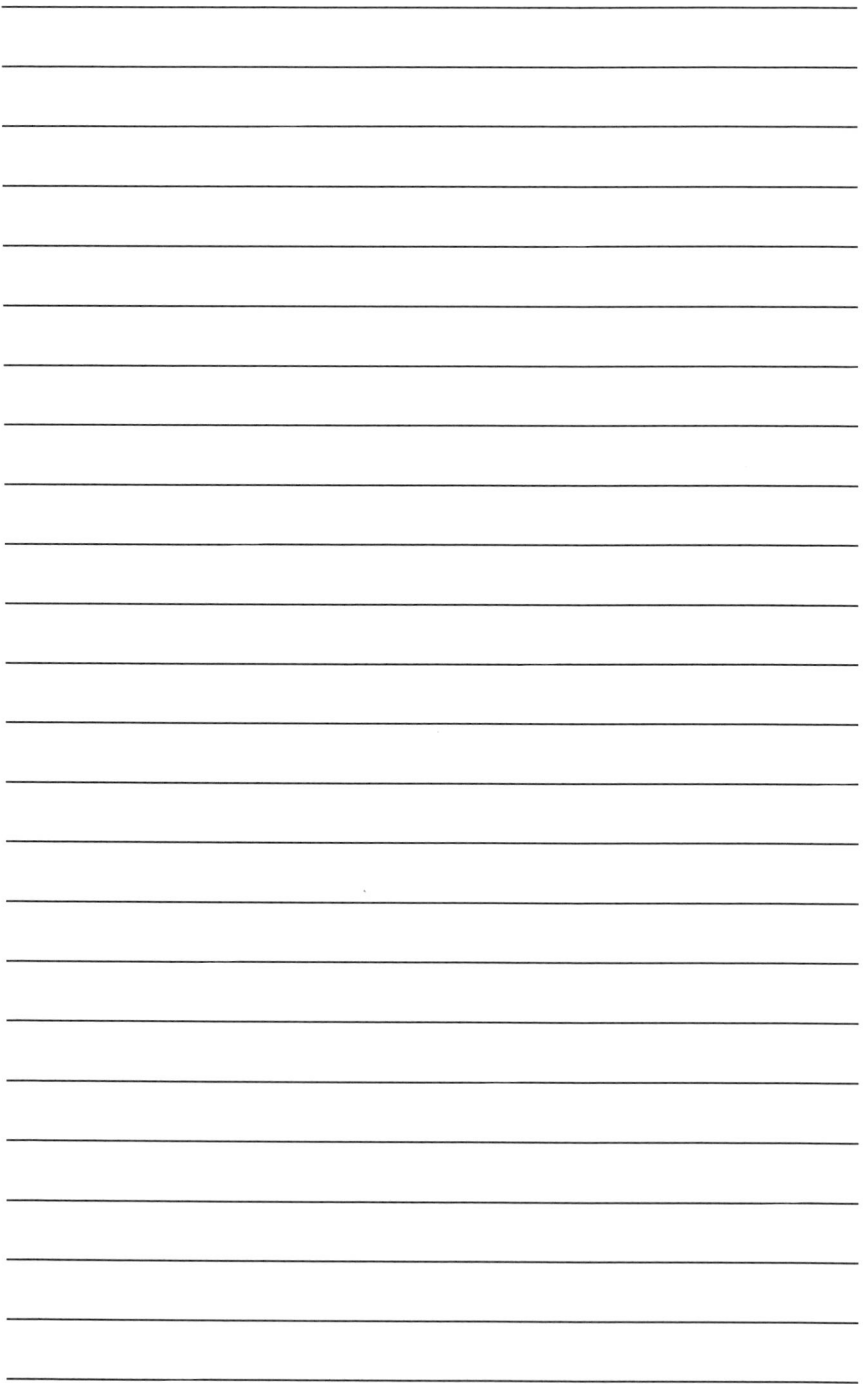

So is my word that goes out from my mouth: It will not return to me empty, but will accomplish what I desire and achieve the purpose for which I sent it.
Isaiah 55:11

Count to 3 as you take a deep breath in and let it out slowly as you count to 7. Sit quietly. Do you see or hear anything? Write your thoughts on the following pages.

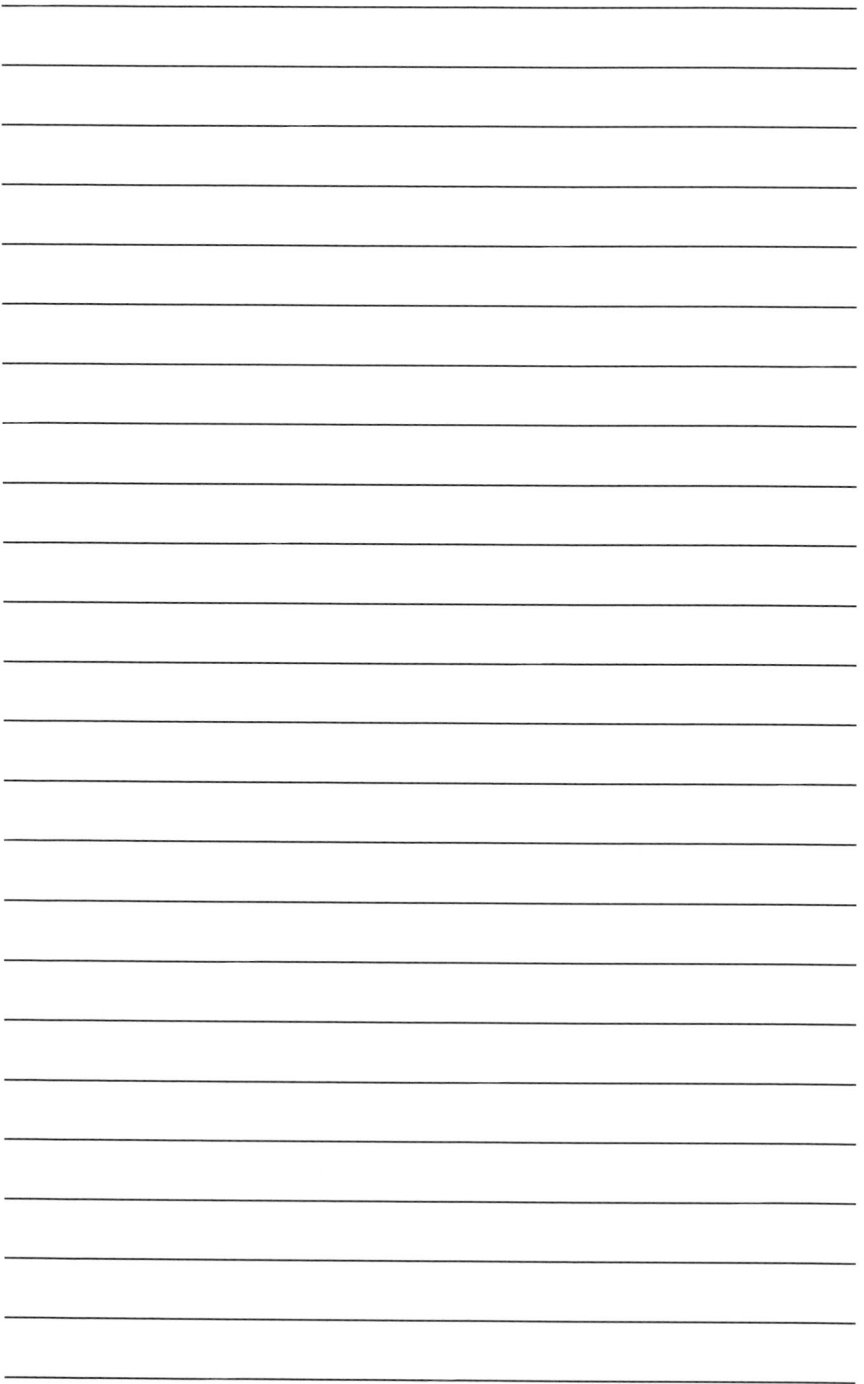

Conclusion

So, there it is.

I wonder what your experience was like...

The more I sit still and pray, listen and see, my mind is blown. The Lord has become so real to me. His presence is real. He truly speaks to us, desires to let us into His secrets. He desires to reveal His mysteries to us. He desires us. It's not easy and we are in process until we are gone but trust that in your surrender there is freedom.

"The LORD bless thee, and keep thee:
The LORD make his face shine upon thee, and be gracious unto thee:
The LORD lift up his countenance upon thee, and give thee peace."
Numbers 6: 24-26

With Love,

Dio <3

Made in the USA
Columbia, SC
06 June 2019